Letter to the Student

IT HAS BEEN BUT A CENTURY AND A SCORE — A MERE EYEBLINK OF TIME

to any historian or philosopher — since psychological science began on a December, 1879, day in Wilhelm Wundt's lab. Since that day we have learned that our neural fabric is composed of separate cells that "talk" to one another through chemical messengers, that our brain's two hemispheres serve differing functions, and that we assemble a simple visual perception by an amazingly intricate process that is rather like taking a house apart, splinter by splinter, and reassembling it elsewhere. We have also learned much about the heritability of various traits, about the roots of misery and happiness, and about the remarkable abilities of newborns. We have learned how abilities vary and how they change with age, how we construct memories, how emotions influence health, how we view and affect one another, and how culture and other environmental factors influence us.

Despite this exhilarating progress, our knowledge may, another century and a score from now, seem to our descendants like relative ignorance. Questions remain unanswered, issues unresolved. What molecular genetics contribute to schizophrenia? What are the relative effects of genetic heritage, home environment, and peers on the personalities and values of developing children? To what extent are our judgments and behaviors the product of thinking that is self-controlled and conscious versus automatic and unconscious? What is the function of dreams? How does the material brain give rise to consciousness?

Psychology is less a set of findings than a way of asking and answering such questions. Over the years, this process of asking and answering questions about behavior and the mind has nowhere been better displayed than in the pages of SCIENTIFIC AMERICAN. In this collection from its recent issues, leading scientists — "Magellans of the mind" — show us how they explore and map the mind. How, from ancient history to the present, have humans understood the brain? How does the brain change with age? How does it enable our perceptions of music, our memories, our language, our intelligence, our disorders? How are we influenced by television, by persuasion, and by our abundance of choices?

In each case, we find a detective story, marked by the testing of competing ideas. "Truth is arrived at by the painstaking process of eliminating the untrue," said master detective Sherlock Holmes. What remains — the apparent truth — is sometimes surprising. "Life is infinitely stranger than anything which the mind of man could invent," Sherlock also declared. So read on, looking not only for the answers, but also for the sleuthing. Therein lies the heart of psychology.

David G. Myers
Hope College
davidmyers.org

Contents

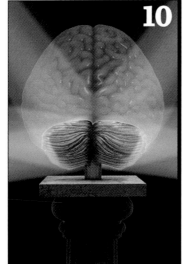
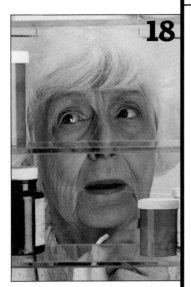

Contents

SENSATION

"Music in Your Head"
by Eckart O. Alternmüller, Scientific American: Mind, 2003

Music, which is part of the universal human experience, is an auditory experience that engages the left hemisphere's processing of rhythm, the right hemisphere's processing of pitch and melody, and combines them with the tactile and emotional experiences processed by other brain areas. For experienced listeners, learning also shapes and supplements the music effect.

DISCUSSION QUESTIONS:

1) What areas of the brain process music?

2) How does learning alter our experience of music?

LANGUAGE

"Sign Language in the Brain"
by Gregory Hickok, Ursula Bellugi, and Edward S. Klima,
Scientific American: The Hidden Mind, 2002

To understand how the brain processes language, some scientists have studied people who hear and speak. But what about people whose language requires seeing and gesture? Gregory Hickok and his colleague explain what leads them to conclude that Deaf signers' and hearing speakers' brains process language similarly. Whether signed or spoken, language processing occurs mostly in the left hemisphere with subfunctions carried out in similar specific areas.

DISCUSSION QUESTIONS:

1) What evidence indicates similarities in how Deaf and hearing people process language?

2) How has brain damage been observed to affect Deaf people's language fluency?

CONSCIOUSNESS

"Television Addiction is No Mere Metaphor"
by Robert Kubey and Mihaly Csikszentmihalyi, Scientific American: Mind, 2003

Many television viewers behave like people with substance dependence: they try and fail to reduce use, and may experience the pain of withdrawal when going cold turkey. Television captures and holds our attention with sudden visual cuts, zooms, pans, and noises that harness our native tendency to orient to any sudden or novel stimulus. But when TV interferes with our active engagement in the "flow" of life, our development and well-being may suffer.

DISCUSSION QUESTIONS:

1) Based on the information in this essay and in your text, would you say that heavy, prolonged TV viewing qualifies as an "addiction?"

2) Do you, or people you know, exhibit a dysfunctional dependence on TV watching? If so, what steps might you or they take to kick the habit or to exert more self-control?

Contents

Contents

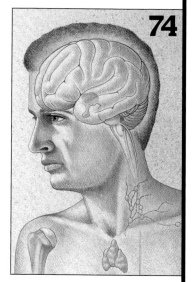

Humbled BY HISTORY

Over the centuries, many "proven" ideas about the brain were later found lacking, a lesson worth remembering today

By Robert-Benjamin Illing

What could have motivated the first *Homo sapiens* to explore the inner life of his head? Incredibly, the earliest evidence we have of such interest reaches back 7,000 years, to skulls from Early Stone Age graves that exhibit carefully cut, man-made holes. These so-called trepanations were performed by various cultures around the world, right up to modern times, and many of the subjects must have survived for years, because their skulls show that scar tissue had formed around the holes.

Ancient cultures presumably practiced trepanation to liberate the soul from the evil spirits that were supposedly responsible for everything from fainting spells to bouts of hysteria. But despite those inquisitions, the philosophers and physicians of old seem to have placed far less importance on the brain and nervous system than on other organs. Both the Bible and the Talmud tell of authentic medical observations, but neither provides a single indi-

The Stone Cutting, by Hieronymus Bosch (circa 1480), depicts a prevalent medieval operation in which a physician removed a "stone of folly" believed to cause mental illness. The words, roughly translated, say: "Master, cut the stone away, I am a simple man."

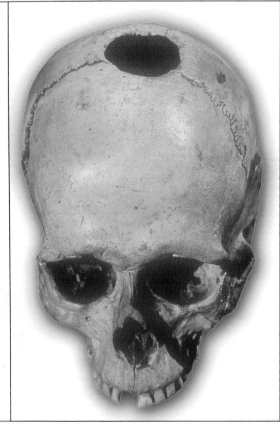

A crater was cut into this human skull from the Mesolithic period, found in Stenghav (Denmark), while its owner was still alive. The edges of the hole have completely healed, which proves that the person survived the operation by years. Such trepanations—attempts to release evil spirits causing illness—were performed up through modern times.

that the brain seemed to be without sensation, for touching the brain of a living animal evoked no response. The action of the heart, he concluded, seemed to correspond with life itself. The soul—the independent force driving that life—most likely resided in the liver.

Unlike Aristotle, Pythagoras (circa 570–496 B.C.) and Hippocrates (circa 460–370 B.C.) both had considered the brain to be the "noblest" part of the body. Plato (427–347 B.C.) shared this point of view. He assigned the lower passions such as lust and greed to the liver and the higher ones such as pride, courage, anger and fear to the heart. For reason, it was the brain.

Galen, the anatomist who lived in Alexandria in about A.D. 130–200, was the first to investigate the brain in earnest. He observed that people who suffered strokes could lose certain senses even though their sensory organs remained intact, inferring that the brain was central to sensation. Galen was especially impressed when he studied the brain's ventricles—the empty spaces—which he believed contained something resembling air. In his experiments, when he pressed on the rear

> Descartes explained that vapors flowed from sensory nerves into the brain's empty spaces, where decisions of the soul pushed them ahead.

cation that any disease was connected to the brain, spinal cord or nerves. The embalmers of Egyptian pharaohs and high priests prepared the liver and heart with great care but removed the brain through the nose and ears using rods and spoons.

As biblical times gave way to the Middle Ages, the Renaissance and our own modern era, more anatomists, physicians and scientists worked hard to understand the complexities of the brain and mind. Yet time and again they had to modify or even discard concepts that their predecessors had formulated after considerable observation and experiment, concepts that once seemed valuable. It is intriguing to wonder which of today's neurological and psychological precepts we may yet have to put aside as we continue to learn more.

In ancient Egypt and Greece, the heart was the most important organ. Greek philosopher Aristotle (384–322 B.C.) noted that an injury to the heart meant immediate death, whereas head injuries usually brought far less serious consequences and could even heal. He observed, too, that one's heartbeat changed with one's emotional state and

ventricle of the exposed brain of a living animal, the animal fell into a deep numbness. If he cut into the ventricle, the animal would not emerge from this trance. If he made only a slight incision into the ventricle surface, the animal would blink its eyes.

Galen also believed there was a special connection between these empty spaces and the soul; after all, the gaseous substance they contained, being ethereal, seemed closer to the soul than brain tissue did. The content of the ventricles was inhaled from the cosmos and served as intermediary between body and soul. He christened the vapors of the ventricles *spiritus animalis*—the "animating spirit"—a concept taken as truth for centuries to come.

A Gentle Breeze

It was a long time before subsequent researchers added to Galen's teachings. In the Middle Ages, people called the ventricles "chambers" and began to assign other functions to them. Like the water in a Roman fountain, the *spiritus animalis* flowed through the ventricles and thereby changed its qualities. This belief was the first timid attempt to create a model of brain function.

During the Renaissance, Leonardo da Vinci (1452–1519) and Michelangelo (1475–1564) sought to learn more about the body by looking inside it. Da Vinci drew the first realistic images showing the brain's ventricles [*see illustration below*]. Flemish anatomist Andreas Vesalius (1514–1564) held celebrated dissections in front of large audiences, carefully preparing and depicting the brain. But no one speculated on how the organ functioned.

This reluctance created an opportunity for René Descartes (1596–1650). The French mathematician and philosopher explained that the visible structures of the brain had nothing to do with its mode of functioning. Influenced by his contemporary, Galileo Galilei (1564–1642), Descartes worked from a mechanistic foundation and transformed the character of brain research. He imagined the *spiritus animalis* as a gentle breeze that flowed from the sensory nerves into the ventricles and then to the brain's central organ, the pineal gland. There the machinelike body—the *res extensa*—encountered the independent, immaterial soul—the *res cogitans*. The decisions of the soul, he maintained, generated impulses that moved through the pineal gland and ventricles, causing the *spiritus animalis* to course through the correct motor nerves to the muscles. Tiny filament valves within the nerve tubes controlled the flow.

Descartes realized that any mechanical system that could control the vast array of sensory and motor events had to be extremely complex. So he devised a new model: a pipe organ. Its air channels corresponded to the heart and arteries, which via the bloodstream carried the *spiritus animalis* to the ventricles. Like organ stops that determined airflow, valves in the nerves helped the *spiritus animalis* flow into the right "pipes." The music was our reasonable and coordinated behavior.

Descartes's theory was so mechanistic that it could be experimentally verified. Italian physician Giovanni Borelli (1608–1679) held a living animal underwater so that it strove with all its power not to drown. According to the theory, *spiritus animalis* ought to have streamed into its muscles. After a few seconds, he cut into a muscle. Because no bubbles rose into the water, he decided that the animating spirit must be watery rather than gaseous— a *succus nerveus* (nerve juice).

Other physicians, anatomists and physicists, including Isaac Newton, conducted experiments to determine how the brain functioned, but their observations produced contradictory results. By the middle of the 18th century a general malaise had spread about knowledge of the brain and nervous system. Could anyone explain how they functioned, even in principle?

Frogs and Sciatic Nerves

New inspiration came from an unlikely place. Everyone inside laboratories and elsewhere was talking about electricity. Some suggested that it was the medium that flowed through the nerves.

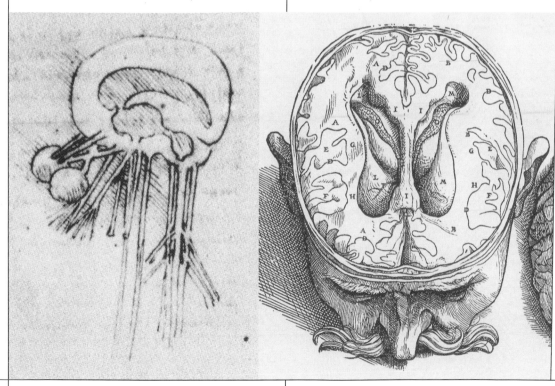

The first anatomically correct representations of the ventricles came from Leonardo da Vinci, whose side view (*left,* circa 1504) shows both the eyeballs and the nerves leading to the brain, and from Andreas Vesalius, who rendered a top view in 1543.

But skeptics noted that nerves seemed to lack insulation. If there was a source of electricity within the body, then the current ought to spread in every direction.

The discussion gained considerable momentum from Italian physician Luigi Galvani (1737–1798). In legendary experiments, he connected a zinc strip to the sciatic nerve of dissected frog legs, then attached the strip with a silver buckle to the muscle. At the moment the circuit was closed and a current flowed, the muscle twitched. The proof that nerves could be stimulated electrically did not, however, prove that electricity and the *spiritus animalis* were identical. It was not until 1843 that German physiologist Emil Du Bois-Reymond (1818–1896) described a current that flowed along a nerve fiber after it was electrically stimulated. When he discovered in 1849 that the same current flowed after chemical stimulation, too, there was finally evidence that the nerves were not passive conductors but producers of electricity.

The question of what nerves were actually made of, however, could not be investigated with the tools available at the time. Throughout the latter 19th century the optics in microscopes were improved, and advances were made in preparing tissue samples for microscopy. Spanish histologist Santiago Ramón y Cajal (1852–1934) noticed that in brain tissue that had been stained, certain cell shapes appeared again and again. He went on to determine that at the end of stained axons there were often special thickenings, so-called terminal buttons. This observation caused him to posit that there was no continuous nerve network, as was believed; instead each neuron was an isolated cell with precisely defined boundaries. In 1906 he shared the Nobel Prize with Camillo Golgi of Italy for their work on the structure of the nervous system. Thus, neuronal theory was born.

Thinking Cells

But how did impulses jump from neuron to neuron? In 1900 Charles Sherrington became the first to demonstrate the existence of inhibitory nerve cells that could turn signals on and off. The English neurophysiologist compared the brain to a telegraph station that sent pulsed messages from point to point. Three years earlier he had already labeled the contact points between neurons "synapses," which literally means "connections." Yet this still did not answer how an impulse could cross a gap. English physiologist John Langley conducted experiments in which he applied nicotine to isolated frog muscles, theorizing that stimulated nerve fibers released a nicotinelike substance at the synapse. But it was German-American chemist and pharmacologist Otto Loewi who finally delivered the experimental proof that a stimulated nerve cell does in fact secrete a substance. His English colleague, Henry Dale, dis-

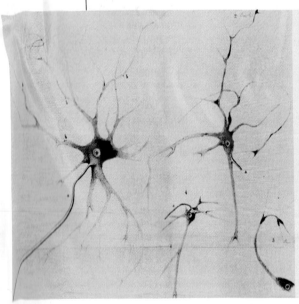

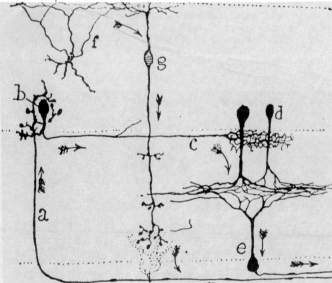

Depictions by German physician Otto Deiters of isolated nerve cells from the spinal cord of an ox (*left*) were the first to distinguish between dendrites and axons. He published them before his untimely death at age 29 in his 1865 book *Investigations on the Brain and Spinal Cord of Man and the Mammals.* Spanish histologist Santiago

Ramón y Cajal was among the earliest to propose that signals travel from neuron to neuron; in one drawing (*right*), he showed the movement of messages via various types of neurons in the retina of a bird, with arrows indicating their directions (from *Histology of the Nervous System of Man and Vertebrates*, 1904).

(Functionalism Refuted?)

A basic tenet of functionalism is that brains and computers are interchangeable. But mathematician and theoretical physicist Roger Penrose of the University of Oxford has used the following thought experiment to shake the theory at its foundation.

All conceivable computers are, in principle, Turing machines (named after English mathematician Alan Turing, who first described them). They carry out sequential operations following definite rules. Turing machines can represent any arbitrary, formal system—one in which each element and each operation is uniquely defined. If the Turing machine is a model for the brain, then brain function is a formal system.

Now consider Austrian-born mathematician Kurt Gödel's incompleteness theorem, or theory of improvability. According to the theorem, in any formal system there are mathematical axioms that are true but that cannot be proved true within the system. Yet if our thoughts constitute a formal system, then we should not be able to recognize the validity of the Gödel axiom. Penrose concluded from this that human capacities of understanding cannot be enclosed within a formal system; the brain is not a Turing machine, and thus the presupposition of functionalism is false. *—R.-B.I.*

---

covered that this substance was acetylcholine.

In parallel, the first recording of an impulse inside a nerve cell—today called an action potential—was made in 1939 by Alan Hodgkin and Andrew Huxley, two English biophysicists. The action potential proved to be the universal signaling mechanism in nerve cells throughout the animal kingdom.

Nevertheless, neuroscientists were slow to embrace the idea of a chemical transmission of nerve impulses until biophysicist Bernhard Katz of University College London and his colleagues showed in the early 1950s that nerve endings secreted signal substances he called neurotransmitters. The molecules were secreted in "packets" depending on the neurons' electrical activity. Finally, in 1977 in the U.S., cell biologists John Heuser and Thomas Reese demonstrated that vesicles in a neuron's cell membrane gave up their contents of neurotransmitters when hit by an incoming action potential. Whether the "sending cell" or the "receiving cell" would be excited or inhibited depended on the neurotransmitter released and the receptor on the membrane to which it bound.

The discovery of excitatory and inhibitory synapses fed speculation that the nervous system processed information according to fixed procedures. But Canadian psychologist Donald O. Hebb had ventured in 1949 that the communication between nerve cells could change depending on the cells' patterns of activity. In recent decades, his suppositions have been experimentally confirmed many times. The intensity of communication between two neurons can be modified by experience. Nerve cells can learn.

That conclusion had enormous implications for theories of how we *Homo sapiens* think. For centuries, the world's scientists had failed to correlate how the brain's parts functioned with how the mind created thought. Even in the Renaissance

it had become clear from observations of diseased and injured people that a person's thinking is inseparable from his or her brain. But what exactly made this organ work? Was it the peculiarities of its neurons, how they were organized, or how they "talked" to one another?

Thomas Willis (1621–1675) had made the first attempts to tie various regions of the brain to specific functions. In his influential work the English doctor declared that the convolutions of the cerebral cortex were the seat of memory and that the white matter within the cerebrum was the seat of the imagination. An area in the interior of the cerebrum—the corpus striatum—was responsible for sensation and motion. Swedish anatomist Emanuel Swedenborg (1688–1772) added that even the outwardly unvarying cerebral cortex must consist of regions with different functions. Otherwise, how could we keep the various aspects of our thoughts separate?

To Map the Brain

The first experimental maps of brain function did not come along until two anatomists in 19th-century Berlin—Eduard Hitzig and Gustav Theodor Fritsch—carefully stimulated the cerebral cortex of cats. Electrically stimulating the rear two thirds of the cortex caused no physical reaction. Stimulating each side of the frontal lobe, however, led to movements of specific limbs. By reducing the current, the researchers could get specific groups of muscles in a given limb to contract. Meanwhile French country doctor Marc Dax documented that aphasics—people who had lost the ability to speak—had often suffered injuries to a distinct

(The Author)
ROBERT-BENJAMIN ILLING is professor of neurobiology and biophysics at the University Clinic in Freiburg, Germany.

Long thought to be solely
the BRAIN'S COORDINATOR of body movement,
THE CEREBELLUM is now known to be active during
a wide variety of cognitive and perceptual activities

Rethinking
the
"Lesser Brain"

By James M. Bower and Lawrence M. Parsons

"In the back of our skulls, perched upon the brain stem under the overarching mantle of the great hemispheres of the cerebrum, is a baseball-sized, bean-shaped lump of gray and white brain tissue. This is the cerebellum, the 'lesser brain.'"

So began, somewhat modestly, the article that in 1958 introduced the cerebellum to the readers of *Scientific American*. Written by Ray S. Snider of Northwestern University, the introduction continued, "In contrast to the cerebrum, where men have sought and found the centers of so many vital mental activities, the cerebellum remains a region of subtle and tantalizing mystery, its function hidden from investigators." But by the time the second *Scientific American* article on the cerebellum appeared 17 years later, author Rodolfo R. Llinás (currently at New York University Medical Center) confidently stated, "There is no longer any doubt that the cerebellum is a central control point for the organization of movement."

Recently, however, the cerebellum's function has again become a subject of debate. In particular, cognitive neuroscientists using powerful new tools of brain imaging have found that the human cerebellum is active during a wide range of activities that are not directly related to movement. Sophisticated cognitive studies have also revealed that damage to specific areas of the cerebellum can cause unanticipated impairments in nonmotor processes, especially in how quickly and accurately people perceive sensory information. Other findings indicate that the cerebellum may play important roles in short-term memory, attention, impulse control, emotion, higher cognition, the ability to schedule and plan tasks, and possibly even in conditions such as schizophrenia and autism. Additional neurobiological experiments—both on the pattern of sensory inputs to the cerebellum and on the ways in which the cerebellum processes that information—also suggest a need to substantially revise current thinking about the function of this organ. The cerebellum has once again become an area of "tantalizing mystery."

It is evening, after a long day at work. I play my favorite CD: Johannes Brahms's second piano concerto. The solemn horn solo in the first two measures flows into the soft crescendo of a piano chord. A wave of memories floods my mind: pictures of the forest around Rottweil, Germany; lines from poems; that day late one summer when I was 16 years old and first discovered the concerto. The conclusion of a particular movement takes my breath away. The pianist gradually increases the tempo and volume and completely expends his energy. I feel a tingling down my spine.

We have all probably at one time or another experienced this sort of thrill from music. When music causes one of these "skin orgasms," the self-reward mechanisms of the limbic system—the brain's emotional core—are active, as is the case when experiencing sexual arousal, eating or taking cocaine. It is conceivable that such self-reward helped to lead ancient peoples to make music. Humans were already constructing the first music-making tools more than 35,000 years ago: percussive instruments, bone flutes and jaw harps. Since then, music, like language, has been part of every culture across the globe.

Some researchers believe that music also conveys a practical evolutionary advantage: it aids in the organization of community life and in the forging of connections among members of one group when disagreements occur with another. Consider forms such as lullabies, work songs for spinning or harvest time, and war marches. In recent decades, youths listen to and play certain types of music as a means of identification and to set themselves apart from other groups.

Still, many questions remain. What happens in the brain when we listen to music? Are there special neural circuits devoted to creating or processing it? Why is an appreciation for music nearly universal? The study of music as a major brain function is relatively new, but researchers are already working on the answers.

Presstimo Nervoso: The Path to the Brain

It is helpful to review how sound reaches the brain. After sound is registered in the ear, the auditory nerve transmits the data to the brain stem. There the information passes through at least four switching stations, which filter the signals, recognize patterns and help to calculate the differences in the sound's duration between the ears to determine the location from which the noise originates. For example, in the first switching area, called the cochlear nucleus, the nerve cells in the ventral, or more forward, section react mainly to individual sounds and generally pass on incoming signals unchanged; the dorsal, or rear, section processes acoustic patterns, such as the beginning and ending points of a stimulus or changes in frequency.

After the switching stations, the thalamus—a structure in the brain that is often referred to as the gateway to the cerebral cortex—either directs information on to the cortex or suppresses it. This gating effect enables us to control our attention selectively so that we can, for instance, pick out one particular instrument from among all the sounds being produced by an orchestra. The auditory nerve pathway terminates at the primary auditory cortex, or Heschl's gyrus, on the top of the temporal lobe. The auditory cortex is split on both sides of the brain.

At this point, the picture grows more complicated, for several reasons. Observations of patients with brain injuries—a common way to gain insights about which areas of the brain are responsible for specific tasks—made over the past decades have been frustratingly varied and occasionally contradictory. Even modern imaging techniques for measuring mental activity in healthy individuals have produced only incomplete explanations of the anatomical and neurophysiological bases for the perception of music. Part of the difficulty stems from the complexity of music itself [*see box on opposite page*]. In addition, the various aspects of music are handled in different, sometimes overlapping regions [*see box on page 28*]. Last, differences among individuals have clouded interpretations of findings.

FAST FACTS
The Perception of Music

1 >> Music is a powerful form of expression that can bring us to tears—or to our feet. Like language, music has been a part of every human culture across the globe. Exactly why is a matter of debate.

2 >> Scientists are piecing together what happens in the brain when someone listens to music. The brain's response involves a number of regions outside the auditory cortex, including areas normally involved in other kinds of thinking.

3 >> The ear has the fewest sensory cells of any sensory organ—3,500 hair cells occupy the ear versus, for example, 100 million photoreceptors in the eye. Yet hearing is remarkably adaptable; even a little practice at the piano can alter mental patterns considerably.

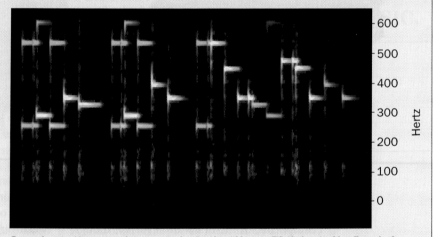

(Dissecting "Happy Birthday")

Imagine we're at a birthday party. With champagne glasses in hand, we strike up what may be the most familiar number of all time: "Happy Birthday to You." We may be thinking we're warbling an uncomplicated tune, but a closer look at this seemingly simple eight-measure song demonstrates how complex and multilayered music actually is.

Music has four types of structures: melodic, temporal, vertical harmonic and dynamic, and each of these categories contains several subcomponents. We can start by listening to the melody as a whole—that is, we can perceive it globally or holistically. We can also break down the melody into separate length-based constituents, starting with the shortest. Taking this local, or analytical, means of perception to the extreme, we may experience the music as its individual tones. If we then put these tones together as a progression, we can consider every so-called interval between each pair.

We can also work within the context of larger temporal-perception units and concentrate on the melody's contours. First, the melody rises somewhat, then falls and rises again in increasingly large steps up to the third "happy birthday to you." At this timescale, the subdivision into antecedent and consequent phrases within a musical period becomes interesting. These phrases adhere to rules of symmetry and harmony and produce a rising tension and then a release. In "Happy Birthday," the antecedent ends shortly before the last, tension-filled jump upward, leading to a softening consequent, from which the melodic line falls away.

In addition to melodies, music has temporal structures, such as rhythm and meter. A rhythm results from the temporal progression of at least three consecutive events. At the beginning of "Happy Birthday," we hear an energetic or punctuated rhythm. This gives the song its festive character, which is underscored by the solid, even progression of quarter notes. The meter is the regular beat, in this case three-four time, which forms the supporting basis for the melody. "Happy Birthday" is not so much a clumsy march but embodies more of the swaying, dancelike character of a minuet or even a waltz. To perceive rhythm and meter, our brains store acoustic events in a temporal context and then recognize how they are arranged.

But there is more to "Happy Birthday" than the horizontal structure made up of melodies, contours, rhythms and meter. Music also has a vertical structure: the timbre and harmony of the individual and multiple tones. The brain perceives all the different elements in milliseconds. The timbre of the birthday party guests' voices as they sing, for example, results from sounds and transient phenomena created by phonation (the production of speech sounds) and by the combination of the singers' harmonics. If we hear the song sung by several voices or with accompaniment, we perceive the harmonies by recognizing the proportion between the number of vibrations in a given time. Simple vibrational proportions generally sound more pleasant to us than the more complex ones. These sensations are subjective: they differ from person to person and from culture to culture and can even change over time.

Finally, when listening to "Happy Birthday," we hear its dynamic structure. The vertical dynamic constitutes volume proportions within a single tone. It arranges the individual voices by their stressing or backing off from the foreground or background of the tone area. The horizontal dynamic describes the volume progression within a group of consecutive tones. This dynamic has a strong effect on the listener's emotions.

One key characteristic of how we hear music is that we can switch among types of perception, only a few of which are described here. We can also quickly become engrossed in the music, thereby again changing the way we are listening. Somehow "Happy Birthday" doesn't sound quite the same anymore.   —E.O.A.

Complex patterns make up music. In the "Happy Birthday to You" melody, a spectrograph's horizontal lines represent the individual tones' frequency spectra (*left to right*). The dynamic structure is represented by color: louder tones are lighter. Octave intervals appear on the left side (*red lines*); at the bottom is the standard pitch A440.

TELEVISION ADDICTION

IS NO MERE METAPHOR

By Robert Kubey and Mihaly Csikszentmihalyi

PHOTOGRAPHS BY CHIP SIMONS

Perhaps the most ironic aspect of the struggle for survival is how easily organisms can be harmed by that which they desire. The trout is caught by the fisherman's lure, the mouse by cheese. But at least those creatures have the excuse that bait and cheese look like sustenance. Humans seldom have that consolation. The temptations that can disrupt their lives are often pure indulgences. No one *has* to drink alcohol, for example. Realizing when a diversion has gotten out of control is one of the great challenges of life.

Islands
OF GENIUS

Artistic brilliance and a dazzling memory can sometimes accompany autism and other developmental disorders

By Darold A. Treffert and Gregory L. Wallace

PHOTOGRAPHS BY ETHAN HILL

Leslie Lemke is a musical virtuoso. At the age of 14 he played, flawlessly and without hesitation, Tchaikovsky's Piano Concerto No. 1 after hearing it for the first time while listening to a television movie several hours earlier. Lemke had never had a piano lesson—and he still has not had one. He is blind and developmentally disabled, and he has cerebral palsy. Lemke plays and sings thousands of pieces at concerts in the U.S. and abroad, and he improvises and composes as well.

Richard Wawro's artwork is internationally renowned, collected by Margaret Thatcher and Pope John Paul II, among others. A London art professor was "thunderstruck" by the oil crayon drawings that Wawro did as a child, describing them as an "incredible phenomenon rendered with the precision of a mechanic and the vision of a poet." Wawro, who lives in Scotland, is autistic.

Kim Peek is a walking encyclopedia. He has memorized more than 7,600 books. He can recite the highways that go to each American city, town or county, along with the area and zip codes, television stations and telephone networks that serve them. If you tell him your date of birth, he can tell you what day of the week it fell on and what day

Kim Peek, who is developmentally disabled, knows more than 7,600 books by heart as well as every area code, highway, zip code and television station in the U.S. He provided the inspiration for the character Raymond Babbitt in the 1988 movie *Rain Man.*

Alonzo Clemons can create perfect wax replicas of any animal he sees, no matter how briefly. His bronze statues are sold by a gallery in Aspen, Colo., and have earned him national repute. Clemons is developmentally disabled.

Decline and Fall of the Roman Empire, by Edward Gibbon, and could recite it back word for word, although he did so without any comprehension.

Although they share many talents, including memory, savants vary enormously in their levels of ability. So-called splinter-skill savants have a preoccupation and mild expertise with, say, the memorization of sports trivia and license plate numbers. Talented savants have musical or artistic gifts that are conspicuously above what would be expected of someone with their handicaps. And prodigious savants are those very uncommon people whose abilities are so advanced that they would be distinctive even if they were to occur in a normal person. Probably fewer than 50 prodigious savants are alive at the moment.

Whatever their talents, savants usually maintain them over the course of their life. With continued use, the abilities are sustained and sometimes even improve. And in almost all cases, there is no dreaded trade-off of these wonderful abilities with the acquisition of language, socialization or daily living skills. Instead the talents often help savants to establish some kind of normal routine or way of life [*see box on next page*].

Looking to the Left Hemisphere

Although specialists today are better able to characterize the talents of savants, no overarching theory can describe exactly how or why savants do what they do. The most powerful explanation suggests that some injury to the left brain causes the right brain to compensate for the loss. The evidence for this idea has been building for several decades. A 1975 pneumoencephalogram study found left hemispheric damage in 15 of 17 autistic patients; four of them had savant skills. (A pneumoencephalogram was an early and painful imaging technique during which a physician would inject air into a patient's spinal fluid and then x-ray the brain to determine where the air traveled. It is no longer used.)

A dramatic study published by T. L. Brink in 1980 lent further credence to the possibility that changes to the left hemisphere were important to savant syndrome. Brink, a psychologist at Crafton Hills College in California, described a normal

nine-year-old boy who had become mute, deaf and paralyzed on the right side when a bullet damaged his left hemisphere. After the accident, unusual savant mechanical skills emerged. He was able to repair multigeared bicycles and to design contraptions, such as a punching bag that would weave and bob like a real opponent.

The findings of Bernard Rimland of the Autism Research Institute in San Diego support this idea as well. Rimland maintains the largest database in the world on people with autism; he has information on more than 34,000 individuals. He has observed that the savant skills most often present in autistic people are those associated with right hemisphere functions and the most deficient abilities are associated with left hemisphere functions.

In the late 1980s Norman Geschwind and Albert M. Galaburda of Harvard University offered an explanation for some causes of left hemispheric damage—and for the higher number of male savants. In their book *Cerebral Lateralization,* the two neurologists point out that the left hemisphere of the brain normally completes its development later than the right and is therefore subject to prenatal influences—some of them detrimental—for a longer period. In the male fetus, circulating testosterone can act as one of these detrimental influences by slowing growth and impairing neuronal function in the more vulnerable left hemisphere. As a result, the right brain often compensates, becoming larger and more dominant in males. The greater male-to-female ratio is seen not just in savant syndrome but in other forms of central nervous system dysfunction, such as dyslexia, delayed speech, stuttering, hyperactivity and autism.

Newly Savant

In recent years, more data have emerged to support the left hemisphere hypothesis. In 1998 Bruce L. Miller of the University of California at San Francisco examined five elderly patients with frontotemporal dementia (FTD), one form of presenile dementia. These patients had developed artistic skills with the onset and progression of their dementia. They were able to make meticulous copies of artworks and to paint beautifully. Consistent with that in savants, the creativity in

> No one knows how savants can do what they do, but research suggests injury to the left brain causes the right brain to compensate.

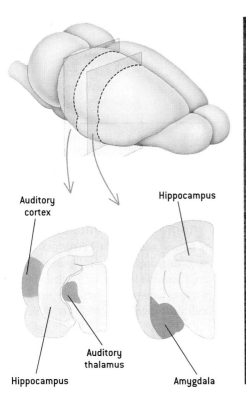

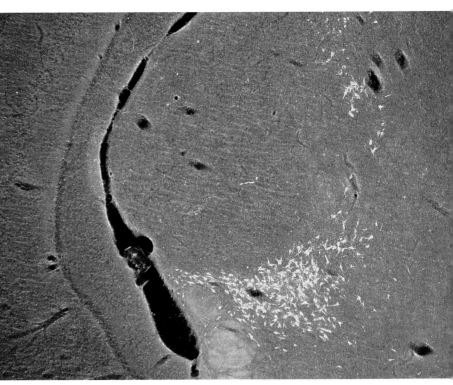

Auditory
cortex

Hippocampus

Hippocampus

Auditory
thalamus

Amygdala

ANATOMY OF EMOTION includes several brain regions. Shown here in the rat, parts of the amygdala, the thalamus and the cortex interact to create memories about fearful experiences, associated here with sound. Work in the past decade has located where fear is learned and remembered: certain parts

eral nucleus can influence the central nucleus via the basolateral nucleus. The lateral nucleus can also influence the central nucleus by way of the accessory basal or basomedial nucleus. Clearly, ample opportunities exist for the lateral nucleus to communicate with the central nucleus once a stimulus has been received.

The emotional significance of such a stimulus is determined by the sound itself and by the environment in which it occurs. Rats must therefore learn not only that a sound or visual cue is dangerous but under what conditions it is so. Russell G. Phillips and I examined the response of rats to the chamber, or context, in which they had been conditioned. We found that lesions of the amygdala interfered with the animals' response to both the tone and the chamber. But lesions of the hippocampus—a brain region involved in declarative memor—interfered only with response to the chamber, not the tone. Declarative memory involves explicit, consciously accessible information, as well as spatial memory. At about the same time, Michael S. Fanselow and Jeansok J. Kim of the University of California at Los Angeles discovered that hippocampal lesions made after fear conditioning had taken place also prevented the expression of responses to the surroundings.

Emotional Significance

THESE FINDINGS were consistent with the generally accepted view that the hippocampus plays an important role in processing complex information, such as details about the spatial environment where activity is taking place. Phillips and I also demonstrated that the subiculum, a region of the hippocampus that projects to other areas of the brain, communicated with the lateral nucleus of the amygdala. This connection suggests that contextual information may acquire emotional significance in the same way that other events do—via transmission to the lateral nucleus.

Although our experiments had identified a subcortical sensory pathway that gave rise to fear conditioning, we did not dismiss the importance of the cortex. The interaction of subcortical and cortical mechanisms in emotion remains a hotly debated topic. Some researchers believe cognition is a vital precursor to emotional experience; others think that cognition—which is presumably a cortical function—is necessary to initiate emotion or that emotional processing is a type of cognitive processing. Still others question whether cognition is necessary for emotional processing.

It became apparent to us that the auditory cortex is involved in, though not crucial to, establishing the fear response, at least when simple auditory stimuli are applied. Norman M. Weinberger and his col-

THE AUTHOR

JOSEPH E. LeDOUX is the Henry and Lucy Moses Professor of Science at New York University. His research is focused on brain mechanisms of emotion and memory. He is the recipient of two National Institute of Mental Health distinctions: a Merit Award and a Research Scientist Development Award. LeDoux's 1996 book, *The Emotional Brain* (Simon & Schuster), was an elaboration of the basic ideas in this *Scientific American* article. His new book, *Synaptic Self* (Viking Penguin), presents a theory of how broad networks in the brain, especially those involved in emotion and memory, are key to understanding the neural basis of personality.

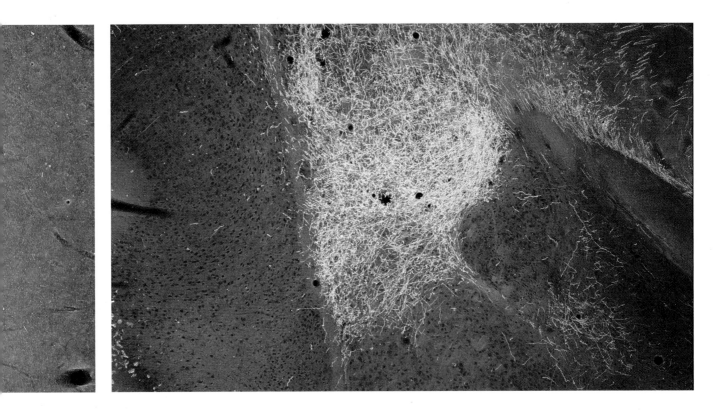

of the thalamus (*pink, left*) communicate with areas in the amygdala (*yellow, right*) that process the fear-causing sound stimuli. These neural mechanisms are thought to be similar in humans, so the study of emotional memory in rodents may illuminate aspects of human fear disorders.

leagues at the University of California at Irvine performed elegant studies showing that neurons in the auditory cortex undergo specific physiological changes in their reaction to sounds as a result of conditioning. This finding indicates that the cortex is establishing its own record of the event.

Experiments by Lizabeth M. Romanski in my laboratory determined that in the absence of the auditory cortex, rats can learn to respond fearfully to a single tone. If, however, projections from the thalamus to the amygdala are removed, projections from the thalamus to the cortex and then to the amygdala are sufficient. Romanski went on to establish that the lateral nucleus can receive input from both the thalamus and the cortex. Her work with rats complements earlier research in primates.

Molecular Mechanisms

ONCE WE HAD a clear understanding of the mechanism through which fear conditioning is learned, we tried to find out how emotional memories are established and stored on a molecular level. Farb and I showed that the excitatory amino acid transmitter glutamate is present in the thalamic cells that reach the lateral nucleus. Chiye J. Aoki and I showed that it is also present at synapses in the lateral nucleus. Because glutamate transmission is implicated in memory formation, we seemed to be on the right track.

Glutamate has been observed in a process called long-term potentiation, or LTP, that has emerged as a model for the creation of memories. This process, which is most frequently studied in the hippocampus, involves a change in the efficiency of synaptic transmission along a neural pathway—in other words, signals travel more readily along this pathway once LTP has taken place. The mechanism seems to involve glutamate transmission and a class of postsynaptic excitatory amino acid receptors known as NMDA (for N-methyl-D-aspartate) receptors.

Various studies have found LTP in the fear-conditioning pathway. Marie-Christine Clugnet and I noted that LTP could be induced in the thalamo-amygdala pathway. Thomas H. Brown and Paul Chapman and their colleagues at Yale discovered LTP in a cortical projection to the amygdala. Other researchers, including Davis and Fanselow, were able to block fear conditioning by blocking NMDA receptors in the amygdala. And Michael T. Rogan in my laboratory found that the processing of sounds by the thalamo-amygdala pathway is amplified after LTP has been induced. The fact that LTP can be demonstrated in a conditioning pathway offers new hope for understanding how LTP might relate to emotional memory.

Studies by Fabio Bordi, also in my laboratory, have suggested hypotheses about what is going on in the neurons of the lateral nucleus during learning. Bordi monitored the electrical state of individual neurons in this area when a rat was listening to the sound and receiving the shock. He and Romanski found that essentially every cell responding to the auditory stimuli also responded to the shock. The basic ingredient of conditioning is thus present in the lateral nucleus.

Bordi was able to divide the acoustically stimulated cells into two classes: habituating and consistently responsive.

Habituating cells eventually stopped responding to the repeated sound, suggesting that they might serve to detect any sound that was unusual or different. They could permit the amygdala to ignore a stimulus once it became familiar. Sound and shock pairing at these cells might reduce habituation, thereby allowing the cells to respond to, rather than ignore, significant stimuli.

The consistently responsive cells had high-intensity thresholds: only loud sounds could activate them. That finding is interesting because of the role volume plays in judging distance. Nearby sounds are presumably more dangerous than those that are far away. Sound coupled with shock might act on these cells to low-er their threshold, increasing the cells' sensitivity to the same stimulus. Consistently responsive cells were also broadly tuned. The joining of a sound and a shock could make the cells responsive to a narrower frequency range or could shift the tuning toward the frequency of the stimulus. Weinberger has shown that cells in the auditory system do alter their tuning to approximate the conditioned stimulus. Bordi and I detected this effect in lateral nucleus cells as well.

The apparent permanence of these memories raises an important clinical question: Can emotional learning be eliminated, and, if not, how can it be toned down? It appears to be quite difficult to get rid of emotional memories, and at best we can hope only to keep them under wraps. Studies by Maria A. Morgan in my laboratory have illuminated how the brain regulates emotional expressions. Morgan showed that when part of the prefrontal cortex is damaged, emotional memory is very hard to extinguish. This discovery indicates that the prefrontal areas—possibly by way of the amygdala—normally control expression of emotional memory and prevent emotional responses once they are no longer useful. A similar conclusion was proposed by Edmund T. Rolls and his colleagues at the University of Oxford during primate studies. The researchers studied the electrical activity of neurons in the frontal cortex of the animals.

The apparent permanence of these memories raises an important CLINICAL QUESTION: Can emotional memory be eliminated?

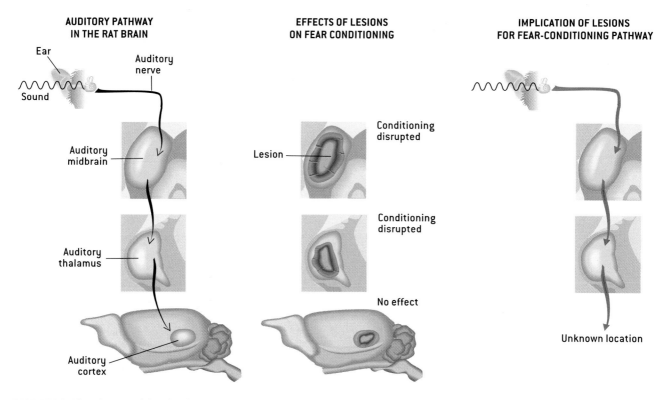

AUDITORY PATHWAY IN THE RAT BRAIN

Ear
Auditory nerve
Sound
Auditory midbrain
Auditory thalamus
Auditory cortex

EFFECTS OF LESIONS ON FEAR CONDITIONING

Lesion
Conditioning disrupted
Conditioning disrupted
No effect

IMPLICATION OF LESIONS FOR FEAR-CONDITIONING PATHWAY

Unknown location

BRAIN LESIONS have been crucial to pinpointing the sites involved in experiencing and learning about fear. When a sound is processed by the rat brain, it follows a pathway from ear to midbrain to thalamus to cortex (*left*). Lesions can be made in various sites in the auditory pathway to determine which areas are necessary for fear conditioning (*center*). Only damage to the cortex does not disrupt the fear response, which suggests that some other areas of the brain receive the output of the thalamus and are involved in establishing memories about experiences that stimulate fear (*right*).

CREATION OF MEMORY has been linked to a process called long-term potentiation, or LTP, in which the neurotransmitter glutamate and its NMDA (for *N*-methyl-D-aspartate) receptors bring about strengthened neural transmission. Once LTP is established, the same neural signals produce larger responses (*right*). Emotional memories may also involve LTP in the amygdala. Glutamate (*red circle in top micrograph*) and NMDA receptors (*red circle in bottom micrograph*) have been found in the region of the amygdala where fear conditioning takes place.

Functional variation in the pathway between this region of the cortex and the amygdala may make it more difficult for some people to change their emotional behavior. Davis and his colleagues found that blocking NMDA receptors in the amygdala interferes with extinction, which hints that it is an active learning process. Such learning could be situated in connections between the prefrontal cortex and the amygdala. More experiments should disclose the answer.

Placing a basic emotional memory process in the amygdalic pathway yields obvious benefits. The amygdala is a critical site of learning because of its central location between input and output stations. Each route that leads to the amygdala—sensory thalamus, sensory cortex and hippocampus—delivers unique information. Pathways originating in the sensory thalamus provide only a crude perception of the external world, but because they involve only one neural link, they are quite fast. In contrast, pathways from the cortex offer detailed and accurate representations, allowing us to recognize an object by sight or sound. But these pathways, which run from the thalamus to the sensory cortex to the amygdala, involve several neural links. And each link in the chain adds time.

Conserving time may be the reason there are two routes—one cortical and one subcortical—for emotional learning. Animals, and humans, need a quick-and-dirty reaction mechanism. The thalamus activates the amygdala at about the same time as it activates the cortex. The arrangement may enable emotional responses to begin in the amygdala before we completely recognize what it is we are reacting to or what we are feeling.

The thalamic pathway may be particularly useful in situations requiring a rapid response. Failing to respond to danger is more costly than responding inappropriately to a benign stimulus. For instance, the sound of rustling leaves is enough to alert us when we are walking in the woods without our first having to identify what is causing the sound. Similarly, the sight of a slender curved shape lying flat on the path ahead of us is sufficient to elicit defensive fear responses [*see illustration on page 59*]. We do not need to go through a detailed analysis of whether or not what we are seeing is a snake. Nor do we need to identify the snake as a reptile or note that its skin can be used to make belts and boots. All these details are irrelevant and, in fact, detrimental to an efficient, speedy and potentially lifesaving reaction. The brain simply needs to be able to store primitive cues and detect them. Later, coordination of this basic information with the cortex permits verification (yes, this is a snake) or brings the response (screaming, sprinting) to a stop.

Storing Emotional Memory

ALTHOUGH THE AMYGDALA stores primitive information, we should not consider it the only learning center. The establishment of memories is a function of the entire network, not just of one component. The amygdala is certainly crucial, but we must not lose sight of the fact that its functions exist only by virtue of the system to which it belongs.

Memory is generally thought to be the process by which we bring back to mind some earlier conscious experience. The original learning and the remembering, in this case, are both conscious events. Researchers have determined that declarative memory is mediated by the hippocampus and the cortex. But removal of the hippocampus has little effect on fear conditioning—except conditioning to context.

In contrast, emotional learning that comes through fear conditioning is not declarative learning. Rather it is mediated by a different system, which may operate independently of conscious awareness. Emotional information may be

PRESYNAPTIC NEURON

Glutamate

POSTSYNAPTIC NEURON

NMDA receptor

Before LTP

After LTP

Neural Impulse (millivolts)

Time (milliseconds)

0   10   20

IAN WORPOLE (*illustrations*); JOSEPH E. LeDOUX (*micrographs*)

stored within declarative memory, but it is kept there as a cold declarative fact. For example, if a person is injured in an auto accident in which the horn gets stuck, he or she may later react when hearing the blare of car horns. The person may remember the details of the accident, such as where and when it occurred and who was involved. These are declarative memories that are dependent on the hippocampus. The individual may also become tense, anxious and depressed as the emotional memory is reactivated through the amygdalic system. The declarative system has stored the emotional content of the experience, but it has done so as a fact.

Emotional and declarative memories are stored and retrieved in parallel, and their activities are joined seamlessly in our conscious experience. That does not mean that we have direct conscious access to our emotional memory; it means instead that we have access to the consequences—such as the way we behave or the way our bodies feel. These consequences combine with current declarative memory to form a new declarative memory. Emotion is not just unconscious memory: it exerts a powerful influence on declarative memory and other thought processes. As James L. McGaugh and his colleagues at the University of California at Irvine have convincingly shown, the amygdala plays an essential part in modulating the storage and strength of memories.

The distinction between declarative memory and emotional memory is an important one. W. J. Jacobs of the University of British Columbia and Lynn Nadel of the University of Arizona have argued that we are unable to remember traumatic early-life events because the hippocampus has not yet matured enough to consciously form accessible memories. The emotional memory system, which may develop earlier, clearly forms and stores its unconscious memories of these events. For this reason, the trauma may affect

Emotion is not just unconscious memory: it exerts a POWERFUL INFLUENCE on declarative memory and other THOUGHT PROCESSES.

mental and behavioral functions in later life through processes that remain inaccessible to consciousness.

Because pairing a tone and a shock can bring about conditioned responses in animals throughout the phyla, it is clear that fear conditioning cannot be dependent on consciousness. Fruit flies and snails, for example, are not creatures known for their conscious mental processes. My way of interpreting this phenomenon is to consider fear a subjective state of awareness brought about when brain systems react to danger. Only if the organism possesses a sufficiently advanced neural mechanism does conscious fear accompany bodily response. This is not to say that only humans experience fear but, rather, that consciousness is a prerequisite to subjective emotional states.

Thus, emotions or feelings are conscious products of unconscious processes. It is crucial to remember that the subjective experiences we call feelings are not the primary business of the system that generates them. Emotional experiences are the result of triggering systems of behavioral adaptation that have been preserved by evolution. Subjective experience of any variety is challenging turf for scientists. We have, however, gained understanding about the neural system that underlies fear responses. This same system may give rise to subjective feelings of fear.

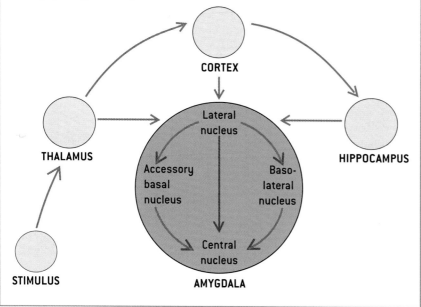

Structure of the Amygdala

THE AMYGDALA plays an important role in emotional behavior. Experiments in rodents have elucidated the structures of various regions of the amygdala and their role in learning about and remembering fear. The lateral nucleus receives inputs from sensory regions of the brain and transmits these signals to the basal, the accessory basal and the central nuclei. The central nucleus connects to the brain stem, bringing about physiological changes.   —J.E.LED.

CORTEX

THALAMUS

STIMULUS

Lateral nucleus

Accessory basal nucleus

Baso-lateral nucleus

Central nucleus

AMYGDALA

HIPPOCAMPUS

If so, studies of the neural control of emotional responses may also hold the key to understanding subjective emotion.

Postscript

MUCH HAS HAPPENED in the study of emotion, memory and the brain since this article was written in 1994, some of which I will summarize.

Additional studies have extended our understanding of the anatomical organization of the amygdala. This work affirms the importance of the lateral nucleus as the gateway into the amygdala and further suggests that information processing occurs at the level of subregions with the lateral nucleus. The importance of the subregional organization of the lateral amygdala is also emphasized by studies in which the activity of neurons has been recorded in response to a tone conditioned stimulus (CS) before and after fear conditioning. The results showed that the CS-elicited activity in the dorsal subnucleus of the lateral amygdala increases dramatically through pairing of the CS with the foot-shock unconditioned stimulus and that different populations of cells in this area are involved in initial learning and in memory storage. Because the cellular activity is learned before fear is expressed, the cellular changes are a plausible part of the explanation of how fear behavior is learned and remembered.

The molecular mechanisms underlying fear learning and memory have been pursued through studies of LTP in brain slices of the lateral amygdala. This work suggests that the induction of LTP can take place by either of two mechanisms. Both of these mechanisms require the influx of calcium into lateral amygdala cells that are postsynaptic—that is, on the receiving end of the signal—to the sensory input pathways. One form of LTP involves calcium entry through voltage-gated calcium channels; the other involves NMDA receptors. Both of these are cellular pathways that, when opened, allow calcium ions to enter the cell. Other studies showed that in live animals, fear conditioning, like LTP, depends on NMDA receptors and the voltage-gated calcium channels. Also, fear conditioning alters neural activity in the lateral amygdala in a manner that closely resembles what happens when LTP is induced in this region, suggesting that LTP is a plausible model of learning.

The elevation of calcium that occurs in postsynaptic neurons during LTP and fear learning triggers a cascade of other chemical processes that leads to a sustained state of enhanced synaptic efficacy between the pre- and postsynaptic neurons. This is a cellular definition of memory. For fear conditioning and many other forms of learning in various species, elevated calcium activates catalytic enzymes called protein kinases (MAP kinase and protein kinase A, among others). These kinases then travel to the cell nucleus, where they activate gene transcription factors (such as CREB), which initiate the synthesis of RNA and proteins. The proteins then travel back to the previously active synapses and stabilize the connection. Because similar molecular steps are involved in different forms of memory in different species, it seems that the uniqueness of different kinds of memory has less to do with the underlying molecules than with the circuits in which they act.

Protein synthesis is not only involved in the initial formation of the memory of an aversive experience but is also called into play when these memories are recalled, which suggests that each time such a memory is activated it has to be restored (reconsolidated) by new protein synthesis. This may be a process by which memories are updated in light of experiences that occurred after the initial memory.

Stimulated by progress in rodent studies, researchers have begun to examine fear processing in the human brain.

MEMORIES of disturbing experiences form deep within our brains.

Studies of patients with damage to the amygdala have shown that this region is required for fear conditioning and other aspects of emotional memory. And functional imaging has shown that the human amygdala is activated during fear conditioning, even under conditions where the CS is prevented from entering consciousness, showing that fear memories can be established unconsciously.

Emotions and memory contribute significantly to our personality, our self. With so much progress made in understanding the brain mechanisms of emotion and memory, we can hope that new research will turn more toward questions about how these factors interact in the shaping of personality, an important topic that neuroscientists have not considered in much detail so far. ⓢⓐ

MORE TO EXPLORE

The Emotional Brain: The Mysterious Underpinnings of Emotional Life. Joseph E. LeDoux. Simon & Schuster, 1998.

Fear Memories Require Protein Synthesis in the Amygdala for Reconsolidation after Retrieval. K. Nader, G. E. Schafe and J. E. LeDoux in *Nature*, Vol. 406, pages 722–726; August 17, 2000.

Perceiving Emotion: There's More Than Meets the Eye. A. K. Anderson and E. A. Phelps in *Current Biology*, Vol. 10, No. 15, pages R551–R554; August 10, 2000.

The Amygdala: Vigilance and Emotion. M. Davis and P. J. Whalen in *Molecular Psychiatry*, Vol. 6, No. 1, pages 13–34; January 2001.

Neurobiology of Pavlovian Fear Conditioning. S. Maren in *Annual Review of Neuroscience*, Vol. 24, pages 897–931; 2001.

Synaptic Self: How Our Brains Become Who We Are. Joseph LeDoux. Viking Penguin, 2002.

The Tyranny of Choice

Logic suggests that having options allows people to select precisely what makes them happiest. But, as studies show, abundant choice often makes for misery

By Barry Schwartz

Americans today choose among more options in more parts of life than has ever been possible before. To an extent, the opportunity to choose enhances our lives. It is only logical to think that if some choice is good, more is better; people who care about having infinite options will benefit from them, and those who do not can always just ignore the 273 versions of cereal they have never tried. Yet recent research strongly suggests that, *psycho*logically, this assumption is wrong. Although some choice is undoubtedly better than none, more is not always better than less.

This evidence is consistent with large-scale social trends. Assessments of well-being by various social scientists—among them, David G. Myers of Hope College and Robert E. Lane of Yale University—reveal that increased choice and increased affluence have, in fact, been accompanied by *decreased* well-being in the U.S. and most other affluent societies. As the gross domestic product more than doubled in the past 30 years, the proportion of the population describing itself as "very happy" declined by about 5 percent, or by some 14 million people. In addition, more of us than ever are clinically depressed. Of course, no one believes that a single factor explains decreased well-being, but a number of findings indicate that the explosion of choice plays an important role.

Thus, it seems that as society grows wealthier and people become freer to do whatever they want, they get less happy. In an era of ever greater personal autonomy, choice and control, what could account for this degree of misery?

Along with several colleagues, I have recently conducted research that offers insight into why many people end up unhappy rather than pleased when their options expand. We began by making a distinction between "maximizers" (those who always aim to make the best possible choice) and "satisficers" (those who aim for "good enough," whether or not better selections might be out there). We borrowed the term "satisficers" from the late Nobel Prize–winning psychologist and economist Herbert A. Simon of Carnegie Mellon University.

In particular, we composed a set of statements—the Maximization Scale—to diagnose people's propensity to maximize. Then we had several thousand people rate themselves from 1 to 7 (from "completely disagree"

THE MAXIMIZATION SCALE

THE STATEMENTS BELOW distinguish maximizers from satisficers. Subjects rate themselves from 1 to 7, from "completely disagree" to "completely agree," on each statement. We generally consider people whose average rating is higher than 4 to be maximizers. When we looked at averages from thousands of subjects, we found that about a third scored higher than 4.75 and a third lower than 3.25. Roughly 10 percent of subjects were extreme maximizers (averaging greater than 5.5), and 10 percent were extreme satisficers (averaging lower than 2.5.)   —B.S.

1. Whenever I'm faced with a choice, I try to imagine what all the other possibilities are, even ones that aren't present at the moment.

2. No matter how satisfied I am with my job, it's only right for me to be on the lookout for better opportunities.

3. When I am in the car listening to the radio, I often check other stations to see if something better is playing, even if I am relatively satisfied with what I'm listening to.

4. When I watch TV, I channel surf, often scanning through the available options even while attempting to watch one program.

5. I treat relationships like clothing: I expect to try a lot on before finding the perfect fit.

6. I often find it difficult to shop for a gift for a friend.

7. Renting videos is really difficult. I'm always struggling to pick the best one.

8. When shopping, I have a hard time finding clothing that I really love.

9. I'm a big fan of lists that attempt to rank things (the best movies, the best singers, the best athletes, the best novels, etc.).

10. I find that writing is very difficult, even if it's just writing a letter to a friend, because it's so hard to word things just right. I often do several drafts of even simple things.

11. No matter what I do, I have the highest standards for myself.

12. I never settle for second best.

13. I often fantasize about living in ways that are quite different from my actual life.

to "completely agree") on such statements as "I never settle for second best." We also evaluated their sense of satisfaction with their decisions.

We did not define a sharp cutoff to separate maximizers from satisficers, but in general, we think of individuals whose average scores are higher than 4 (the scale's midpoint) as maximizers and those whose scores are lower than the midpoint as satisficers. People who score highest on the test—the greatest maximizers—engage in more product comparisons than the lowest scorers, both before and after they make purchasing decisions, and they take longer to decide what to buy. When satisficers find an item that meets their standards, they stop looking. But maximizers exert enormous effort reading labels, checking out consumer magazines and trying new products. They also spend more time comparing their purchasing decisions with those of others.

Naturally, no one can check out every option, but maximizers strive toward that goal, and so making a decision becomes increasingly daunting as the number of choices rises. Worse, after making a selection, they are nagged by the alternatives they have not had time to investigate. In the end, they are more likely to make better objective choices than satisficers but get less satisfaction from them. When reality requires maximizers to compromise—to end a search and decide on something—apprehension about what might have been takes over.

We found as well that the greatest maximizers are the least happy with the fruits of their efforts. When they compare themselves with others, they get little pleasure from finding out that they did better and substantial dissatisfaction from finding out that they did worse. They are more prone to experiencing regret after a purchase, and if their acquisition disappoints them, their sense of well-being takes longer to recover. They also tend to brood or ruminate more than satisficers do.

Does it follow that maximizers are less happy in general than satisficers? We tested this by having people fill out a variety of questionnaires known to be reliable indicators of well-being. As might be expected, individuals with high maximization scores experienced less satisfaction with life and were less happy, less optimistic and more depressed than people with low maximization scores. Indeed, those with extreme maximization ratings had depression scores that placed them in the borderline clinical range.

Recipe for Unhappiness

SEVERAL FACTORS EXPLAIN why more choice is not always better than less, especially for maximizers. High among these are "opportunity costs." The quality of any given option cannot be assessed in isolation from its alternatives. One of the "costs" of making a selection is losing the opportunities that a different option would have afforded. Thus, an opportunity cost of vacationing on the beach in Cape Cod might be missing the fabulous restaurants in the Napa Valley. If we assume that opportunity costs reduce the overall desirability of the most preferred choice, then the more alternatives there are, the deeper our sense of loss will be and the less satisfaction we will derive from our ultimate decision.

Lyle Brenner of the University of Florida and his collabora-

FEELINGS EVOKED BY EVER MORE CHOICES

EARLY DECISION-MAKING RESEARCH by Daniel Kahneman and Amos Tversky showed that people respond much more strongly to losses than gains (*depicted schematically in left graph*). Similarly, my co-workers and I believe that feelings of well-being initially rise as choice increases (*blue line in schematic plot, center graph*) but

then level off quickly (good feelings satiate). Meanwhile, although zero choice (*at the* y *axis*) evokes virtually infinite unhappiness, bad feelings escalate (*red line*) as we go from having few choices to many. The net result (*purple line in right graph*) is that, at some point, added choice only decreases happiness. —*B.S.*

REACTIONS TO LOSSES AND GAINS

REACTIONS TO INCREASING CHOICE

tors demonstrated the effects of opportunity costs when they had subjects put a dollar value on subscriptions to magazines or flights from San Francisco to attractive locations. Some attached prices to a single magazine subscription or a single destination. Others attached prices to the same magazine or destination when it was part of a group containing three others. Prices were consistently lower when a given alternative was evaluated as part of a group than when it was evaluated in isolation.

Why might this be so? When you assign a value to, say, *Newsweek,* as part of a group that also contains *People,* the *New Republic* and *Us,* your tendency will be to compare the various magazines. Perhaps you judge *Newsweek* to be more informative than *People* but less entertaining. Each comparison that *Newsweek* wins will be a gain, but each comparison that it loses will be a loss, an opportunity cost. Any particular magazine will both benefit and suffer from comparison with others. But we know from the research of Nobelist psychologist Daniel Kahneman of Princeton University and his late colleague Amos Tversky of Stanford that losses (in this case, opportunity costs) have a much greater psychological impact than gains. Losses make us hurt more than gains make us feel good.

Sometimes opportunity costs may create enough conflict to produce paralysis. For example, participants in one study were offered $1.50 for filling out some questionnaires. After they finished, they were offered a fancy metal pen instead of the $1.50 and told that the pen usually costs about $2. Seventy-five percent chose the pen. In a second condition, subjects were offered the $1.50 or a choice between that same metal pen and a pair of less expensive felt-tipped pens (also worth about $2 together). Now fewer than 50 percent chose any pen.

The problem of opportunity costs will be worse for a max-

imizer than for a satisficer. The latter's "good enough" philosophy can survive thoughts about opportunity costs. In addition, the "good enough" standard leads to much less searching and inspection of alternatives than the maximizer's "best" standard. With fewer choices under consideration, a person will have fewer opportunity costs to subtract.

Regret Adds to Costs

JUST AS PEOPLE FEEL sorrow about the opportunities they have forgone, they may also suffer regret about the option they settle on. My colleagues and I devised a scale to measure proneness to feeling regret, and we found that people with high sensitivity to regret are less happy, less satisfied with life, less optimistic and more depressed than those with low sensitivity. Not surprisingly, we also found that people with high regret sensitivity tend to be maximizers. Indeed, we think that worry over future regret is a major reason that individuals become maximizers. The only way to be sure you will not regret a decision is by making the best possible one. Unfortunately, the more options you have and the more opportunity costs you incur, the more likely you are to experience regret.

Regret may be one reason for our aversion to losses. Have you ever bought an expensive pair of shoes only to discover that they are so uncomfortable that you cannot wear them for more than 10 minutes without hobbling? Did you toss them out, or are they still sitting in the back of your closet? Chances are you had a hard time throwing them away. Having bought the shoes, you incurred an actual, or "sunk," cost, and you are going to keep them around in the hope that eventually you will get your money's worth out of them. To give the shoes away or throw them out would force you to acknowledge a mistake—a loss.

BARRY SCHWARTZ

In a classic demonstration of the power of sunk costs, people were offered season subscriptions to a local theater company. Some were offered the tickets at full price and others at a discount. Then the researchers simply kept track of how often the ticket purchasers actually attended the plays over the course of the season. Full-price payers were more likely to show up at performances than discount payers. The reason for this, the investigators argued, was that the full-price payers would experience more regret if they did not use the tickets because not using the more costly tickets would constitute a bigger loss.

Several studies have shown that two of the factors affecting regret are how much one feels personal responsibility for the result and how easy it is to imagine a better alternative. The availability of choice obviously exacerbates both these factors. When you have no options, what can you do? You will feel disappointment, maybe; regret, no. With no options, you just do the best you can. But with many options, the chances increase that a really good one is out there, and you may well feel that you ought to have been able to find it.

Adaptation Dulls Joy

A PHENOMENON called adaptation also contributes to the fallout we face from too many choices. Simply put, we get used to things, and as a result, very little in life turns out quite as good as we expect it to be. After much anguish, you might decide to buy a Lexus and then try to put all the attractions of other models out of your mind. But once you are driving your new car, adaptation begins, and the experience falls just a little bit flat. You are hit with a double whammy—regret about what you did not choose and disappointment with what you did, even if your final decision was not bad.

Because of adaptation, enthusiasm about positive experi-

THE AUTHOR

BARRY SCHWARTZ is Dorwin Cartwright Professor of Social Theory and Social Action in the department of psychology at Swarthmore College, where he has taught since 1971. He recently published a book on the consequences of excessive choice (see "More to Explore," on opposite page) and has written several other books, including The Battle for Human Nature and The Costs of Living.

Toothpaste! GOOD ENOUGH FLAVOR

LESSONS

Choose when to choose.
We can decide to restrict our options when the decision is not crucial. For example, make a rule to visit no more than two stores when shopping for clothing.

Learn to accept "good enough."
Settle for a choice that meets your core requirements rather than searching for the elusive "best." Then stop thinking about it.

Don't worry about what you're missing.
Consciously limit how much you ponder the seemingly attractive features of options you reject. Teach yourself to focus on the positive parts of the selection you make.

Control expectations.
"Don't expect too much, and you won't be disappointed" is a cliché. But that advice is sensible if you want to be more satisfied with life. —B.S.

ences does not sustain itself. Daniel T. Gilbert of Harvard University and Timothy D. Wilson of the University of Virginia and their collaborators have shown that people consistently mispredict how long good experiences will make them feel good and how long bad experiences will make them feel bad. The waning of pleasure or enjoyment over time always seems to come as an unpleasant surprise.

And it may cause more disappointment in a world of many options than in a world of few. The opportunity costs associated with a decision and the time and effort that go into making it are "fixed costs" that we "pay" up front, and those costs then get "amortized" over the life of the decision. The more we invest in a decision, the more satisfaction we expect to realize from our investment. If the decision provides substantial satisfaction for a long time after it is made, the costs of making it recede into insignificance. But if the decision provides pleasure for only a short time, those costs loom large. Spending four months deciding what stereo to buy is not so bad if you really enjoy that stereo for 15 years. But if you end up being excited by it for six months and then adapting, you may feel like a fool for having put in all that effort.

The Curse of High Expectations

A SURFEIT OF alternatives can cause distress in yet another way: by raising expectations. In the fall of 1999 the *New York Times* and CBS News asked teenagers to compare their experiences with those their parents had growing up. Fifty percent of children from affluent households said their lives were harder. When questioned further, these adolescents talked about high expectations, both their own and their parents'. They talked about "too muchness": too many activities, too many consumer choices, too much to learn. As one commentator put it, "Children feel the pressure ... to be sure they don't slide back. Everything's about going forward.... Falling back is the American nightmare." So if your perch is high, you have much further to fall than if your perch is low.

The amount of choice we now have in most aspects of our lives contributes to high expectations. When I was on vacation a few years ago in a tiny seaside town on the Oregon coast, I went into the local grocery store to buy ingredients for dinner.

MATT COLLINS

The store offered about a dozen options for wine. What I got was so-so, but I did not expect to be able to get something very good and, hence, was satisfied with what I had. If instead I had been shopping in a store that offered an abundance of choices, my expectations would have been a good deal higher and that same so-so wine might have left me sorely disappointed.

Alex C. Michalos of the University of Northern British Columbia has pointed out that all our evaluations of the things we do and buy depend on comparison—to past experiences, to what we were hoping for, and to what we expected. When we say that some experience was good, what we mean, in part, is that it was better than we expected it to be. So high expectations almost guarantee that experiences will fall short, especially for maximizers and especially when regret, opportunity costs, and adaptation do not factor into our expectations.

A Link to Depression?

THE CONSEQUENCES OF unlimited choice may go far beyond mild disappointment, to suffering. As I indicated earlier, Americans are showing a decrease in happiness and an increase in clinical depression. One important contributing factor, I think, is that when we make decisions, experience the consequences and find that they do not live up to expectations, we blame ourselves. Disappointing outcomes constitute a personal failure that could and should have been avoided if only we had made a better choice.

The research that my colleagues and I have done suggests that maximizers are prime candidates for depression. With group after group of people, varying in age (including young adolescents), gender, educational level, geographic location, race and socioeconomic status, we have found a strong correlation between maximizing and measures of depression. If the experience of disappointment is relentless, if virtually every choice you make fails to live up to expectations and aspirations, and if you consistently take personal responsibility for the disappointments, then the trivial looms larger and larger, and the conclusion that you cannot do anything right becomes devastating. Although depression has many sources, and the relation among choice, maximizing and depression requires more study, there is good reason to believe that overwhelming choice at least contributes to the epidemic of unhappiness spreading through modern society.

What Can Be Done

THE NEWS I HAVE reported is not good. We get what we say we want, only to discover that what we want does not satisfy us to the degree that we expect. Does all this mean that we would all be better off if our choices were severely restricted, even eliminated? I do not think so. The relation between choice and well-being is complicated. A life without significant choice would be unlivable. Being able to choose has enormous important positive effects on us. But only up to a point. As the number of choices we face increases, the psychological benefits we derive start to level off. At the same time, some of the negative effects of choice that I have discussed begin to appear, and rather than leveling off, they accelerate. A quarter of a century ago the late

Clyde H. Coombs of the University of Michigan at Ann Arbor and George S. Avrunin of the University of Massachusetts at Amherst noted that good things "satiate" and bad things "escalate." Much the same can be said of feelings. Indeed, a point is reached at which increased choice brings increased misery rather than increased opportunity. It appears that American society has long since passed that point.

Few Americans would favor passing laws to limit choices. But individuals can certainly take steps to mitigate choice-related distress. Such actions require practice, discipline and perhaps a new way of thinking, but each should bring its own rewards [see box on opposite page].

Beyond those individual strategies, I think our society would be well served to rethink its worship of choice. As I write this, public debate continues about privatization of Social Security (so people could select their retirement investments), privatization of Medicare and prescription drug benefits (so people could choose their own health plans), and choice in public education. And in the private sphere, medical ethicists treat the idea of "patient autonomy" as sacrosanct, as if it goes without saying that having patients choose their treatments will make them better off. Software developers design their products so that users can customize them to their own specific needs and tastes, as if the resulting complexity and confusion are always a price worth paying to maximize user flexibility. And manufacturers keep offering new products or new versions of old products, as if we needed more variety. The lesson of my research is that developments in each of these spheres may well rest on assumptions that are deeply mistaken. SA

MORE TO EXPLORE

Choices, Values, and Frames. Daniel Kahneman and Amos Tversky in *American Psychologist*, Vol. 39, pages 341–350; April 1984.

The Loss of Happiness in Market Democracies. Robert E. Lane. Yale University Press, 2001.

Maximizing versus Satisficing: Happiness Is a Matter of Choice. Barry Schwartz, Andrew Ward, John Monterosso, Sonya Lyubomirsky, Katherine White and Darrin Lehman in *Journal of Personality and Social Psychology*, Vol. 83, No. 5, pages 1178–1197; 2002.

The Paradox of Choice: Why More Is Less. Barry Schwartz. Ecco/HarperCollins Publishers, 2004.

MATT COLLINS

The brain and the immune system
continuously signal each other, often along
the same pathways, which may explain
how state of mind influences health

The Mind-Body
Interaction
in Disease

By Esther M. Sternberg and Philip W. Gold

The belief that the mind plays an important role in physical illness goes back to the

earliest days of medicine. From the time of the ancient Greeks to the beginning of the 20th century, it was generally accepted by both physician and patient that the mind can affect the course of illness, and it seemed natural to apply this concept in medical treatments of disease. After the discovery of antibiotics, a new assumption arose that treatment of infectious or inflammatory disease requires only the elimination of the foreign organism or agent that triggers the illness. In the rush to discover antibiotics and drugs that cure specific infections and diseases, the fact that the body's own responses can influence susceptibility to disease and its course was largely ignored by medical researchers.

It is ironic that research into infectious and inflammatory disease first led 20th-century medicine to reject the idea that the mind influences physical illness, and now research in the same field—including the work of our laboratories and of our collaborators at the National Institutes of Health—is proving the contrary. New molecular and pharmacological tools have made it possible for us to identify the intricate network that exists between the immune system and the brain, a network that allows the two systems to signal each other continuously and rapidly. Chemicals produced by immune cells signal the brain, and the brain in turn sends chemical signals to restrain the immune system. These same chemical signals also affect behavior and the response to stress. Disruption of this communication network in any way, whether inherited or through drugs,

toxic substances or surgery, exacerbates the diseases that these systems guard against: infectious, inflammatory, autoimmune, and associated mood disorders.

The clinical significance of these findings is likely to prove profound. They hold the promise of extending the range of therapeutic treatments available for various disorders, as drugs previously known to work primarily for nervous system problems are shown to be effective against immune maladies, and vice versa. They also help to substantiate the popularly held impression (still discounted in some medical circles) that our state of mind can influence how well we resist or recover from infectious or inflammatory diseases.

The brain's stress response system is activated in threatening situations. The immune system responds automatically to pathogens and foreign molecules. These two response systems are the body's principal means for maintaining an internal steady state called homeostasis. A substantial proportion of human cellular machinery is dedicated to maintaining it.

When homeostasis is disturbed or threatened, a repertoire of molecular, cellular and behavioral responses comes into play. These responses attempt to counteract the disturbing forces in order to reestablish a steady state. They can be specific to the foreign invader or a particular stress, or they can be generalized and nonspecific when the threat to homeostasis exceeds a certain threshold. The adaptive responses may themselves

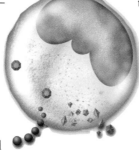

IMMUNE RESPONSE can be
altered at the cellular level
by stress hormones.

Updated from The Mysteries of the Mind *(Special Issue, 1997)*

ANATOMY OF THE STRESS AND IMMUNE SYSTEMS

STRESS RESPONSE

Nerves connect the brain to every organ and tissue. Challenging or threatening situations activate the brain's stress response, which involves the release of a hormone that stimulates physiological arousal and regulates the immune system. Key components in this stress response are the hypothalamus and locus ceruleus in the brain, the pituitary gland, the sympathetic nervous system and the adrenal glands.

IMMUNE RESPONSE

The immune system operates as a decentralized network, responding automatically to anything that invades or disrupts the body. Immune cells generated in the bone marrow, lymph nodes, spleen and thymus communicate with one another using small proteins. These chemical messengers can also send signals to the brain, through either the bloodstream or through nerve pathways such as the vagus nerve to the nucleus of the tractus solitarius.

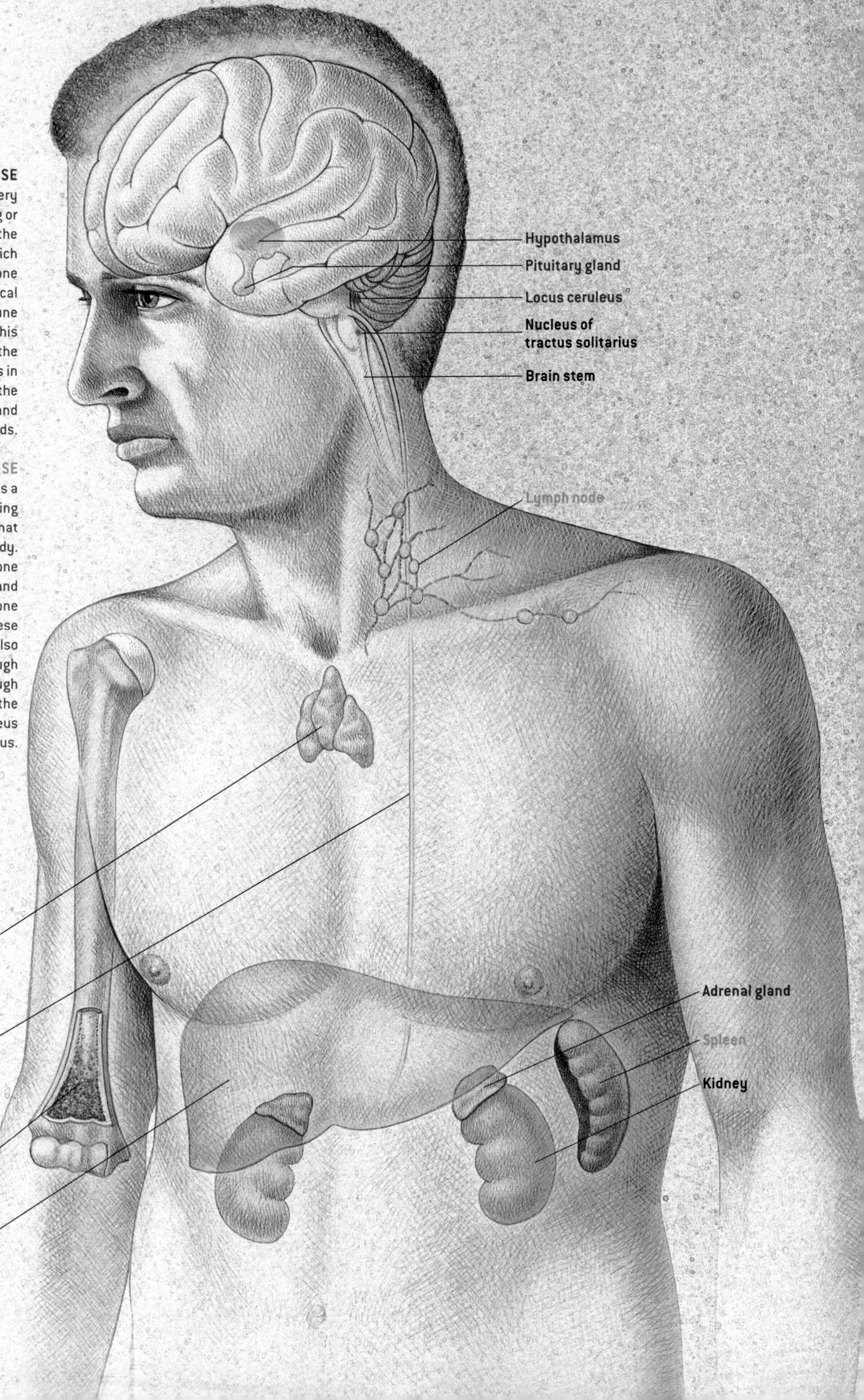

Hypothalamus

Pituitary gland

Locus ceruleus

Nucleus of tractus solitarius

Brain stem

Lymph node

Thymus

Vagus nerve

Bone marrow

Liver

Adrenal gland

Spleen

Kidney

turn into stressors capable of producing disease. We are just beginning to understand the interdependence of the brain and the immune system, how they help to regulate and counterregulate each other and how they themselves can malfunction and produce disease.

The stress response promotes physiological and behavioral changes in threatening or taxing situations. For instance, when we are facing a potentially life-threatening situation, the brain's stress response goes into action to enhance our focused attention, our fear and our fight-or-flight response, while inhibiting behaviors, such as feeding, sex and sleep, that might lessen the chance of immediate survival. The stress response, however, must be

The central nervous and immune systems, however, are more similar than different in their modes of receiving, recognizing and integrating various signals and in their structural design for accomplishing these tasks. Both the central nervous system and the immune system possess "sensory" elements, which receive information from the environment and other parts of the body, and "motor" elements, which carry out an appropriate response.

Cross Communication

BOTH SYSTEMS also rely on chemical mediators for communication. Electrical signals along nerve pathways, for instance, are converted to chemical signals at the synapses between neurons. The

to the pituitary gland, which lies just beneath the brain. CRH causes the pituitary to release adrenocorticotropin hormone (ACTH) into the bloodstream, which stimulates the adrenal glands to produce cortisol, the best-known stress hormone.

Cortisol is a steroid hormone that increases the rate and strength of heart contractions, sensitizes blood vessels to the actions of norepinephrine (an adrenaline-like hormone) and affects many metabolic functions—actions that help the body meet a stressful situation. In addition, cortisol is a potent immunoregulator and anti-inflammatory agent. It plays a crucial role in preventing the immune system from overreacting to injuries and damaging tissues. Furthermore, cortisol inhibits

The ADAPTIVE RESPONSES may themselves turn into stressors capable of PRODUCING DISEASE.

regulated to be neither excessive nor suboptimal; otherwise, disorders of arousal, thought and feeling emerge.

The immune system's job is to bar foreign pathogens from the body and to recognize and destroy those that penetrate its shield. The immune system must also neutralize potentially dangerous toxins, facilitate repair of damaged or worn tissues, and dispose of abnormal cells. Its responses are so powerful that they require constant regulation to ensure that they are neither excessive nor indiscriminate and yet remain effective. When the immune system escapes regulation, autoimmune and inflammatory diseases or immune deficiency syndromes result.

The immune and central nervous systems appear, at first glance, to be organized in very different ways. The brain is usually regarded as a centralized command center, sending and receiving electrical signals along fixed pathways, much like a telephone network. In contrast, the immune system is decentralized, and its organs (spleen, lymph nodes, thymus and bone marrow) are located throughout the body. The classical view is that the immune system communicates by releasing immune cells into the bloodstream that travel to new locations to deliver their messages or to perform other functions.

chemical messengers produced by immune cells communicate not only with other parts of the immune system but also with the brain and nerves. Chemicals released by nerve cells can act as signals to immune cells. Hormones from the body travel to the brain in the bloodstream, and the brain itself makes hormones. Indeed, the brain is perhaps the most prolific endocrine organ in the body and produces many hormones that act both on the brain and on tissues throughout the body.

A key hormone shared by the central nervous and immune systems is corticotropin-releasing hormone (CRH); produced in the hypothalamus and several other brain regions, it unites the stress and immune responses. The hypothalamus releases CRH into a specialized bloodstream circuit that conveys the hormone

the release of CRH by the hypothalamus—which keeps this component of the stress response under control. Thus, CRH and cortisol directly link the body's brain-regulated stress response and its immune response.

CRH-secreting neurons of the hypothalamus send fibers to regions in the brain stem that help to regulate the sympathetic nervous system, as well as to another brain stem area called the locus ceruleus. The sympathetic nervous system, which mobilizes the body during stress, also innervates immune organs, such as the thymus, lymph nodes and spleen, and helps to control inflammatory responses throughout the body. Stimulation of the locus ceruleus leads to behavioral arousal, fear and enhanced vigilance.

Perhaps even more important for the

THE AUTHORS

ESTHER M. STERNBERG and PHILIP W. GOLD carry out their research on stress and immune systems at the National Institute of Mental Health. Sternberg is chief of the section on neuroendocrine immunology and behavior and director of the Integrative Neural Immune Program, and Gold is chief of the clinical neuroendocrinology branch. Sternberg received her M.D. from McGill University. Her work on the mechanisms and molecular basis of neural immune communication has led to a growing recognition of the importance of mind-body interaction. She is also the author of The Balance Within: The Science Connecting Health and Emotions (2000). Before joining the NIMH in 1974, Gold received his medical training at Duke University and Harvard University. He and his group were among the first to introduce data implicating corticotropin-releasing hormone and its related hormones in the pathophysiology of melancholic and atypical depression and in the mechanisms of action of antidepressant drugs.

induction of fear-related behaviors is the amygdala, where inputs from the sensory regions of the brain are charged as stressful or not. CRH-secreting neurons in the central nucleus of the amygdala send fibers to the hypothalamus, the locus ceruleus, and to other parts of the brain stem. These CRH-secreting neurons are targets of messengers released by immune cells during an immune response. By recruiting the CRH-secreting neurons, the immune signals not only activate cortisol-mediated restraint of the immune response but also induce behaviors that assist in recovery from illness or injury. CRH-secreting neurons also have connections with hypothalamic regions that regulate food intake and reproductive behavior. In addition, other hormonal and nerve systems—such as the thyroid, growth and female sex hormones, and the sympathomedullary pathways (connections of the sympathetic nervous system and medulla)—influence interactions between the brain and the immune system.

Immune System Signals

THE IMMUNE RESPONSE is an elegant and finely tuned cascade of cellular events aimed at ridding the body of foreign substances, bacteria and viruses. One of the major discoveries of contemporary immunology is that white blood cells produce small proteins that indirectly coordinate the responses of other parts of the immune system to pathogens.

For example, the protein interleukin-1 (IL-1) is made by a type of white blood cell called a monocyte or macrophage. IL-1 stimulates another type of white blood cell, the lymphocyte, to produce interleukin-2 (IL-2), which in turn induces lymphocytes to develop into mature immune cells. Some mature lymphocytes, called plasma cells, make antibodies that fight infection, whereas others, the cytotoxic lymphocytes, kill viruses directly. Other interleukins mediate the activation of immune cells that are involved in allergic reactions.

The interleukins were originally named for what was considered to be their primary function: communication among ("inter-") the white blood cells ("leukins"). But interleukins also act as chemical signals among immune cells and many other types of cells and organs, including parts of the brain. Cytokines is the more general term for biological molecules that many different kinds of cells use to communicate. Each cytokine is a distinct protein molecule, encoded by a separate gene, that targets a particular cell type. A cytokine can either stimulate or inhibit a response depending on the presence of other cytokines or other stimuli and the current state of metabolic activity. This flexibility allows the immune system to take the most appropriate actions to stabilize the local cellular environment and to maintain homeostasis.

Cytokines from the body's immune system can send signals to the brain in several ways. Ordinarily, a "blood-brain barrier" shields the central nervous system from potentially dangerous molecules in the bloodstream. During inflammation or illness, however, this barrier becomes more permeable, and cytokines may be carried across into the brain with nutrients from the blood. Certain cytokines, on the other hand, readily pass through leaky areas in the blood-brain barrier at any time. But cytokines do not have to cross the blood-brain barrier to exert their effects. Cytokines can attach to their receptors in the lining of blood vessels in the brain and stimulate the release of secondary chemical signals in the brain tissue around the blood vessels.

Cytokines can also signal the brain via direct nerve routes, such as the vagus nerve, which innervates the heart, stomach, small intestine and other organs of the abdominal cavity. Injection of IL-1 into the abdominal cavity activates the nucleus of the tractus solitarius, the principal region of the brain stem for receipt of visceral sensory signals. Cutting the vagus nerve blocks activation of this brain

STRESS RESPONSE SYSTEM

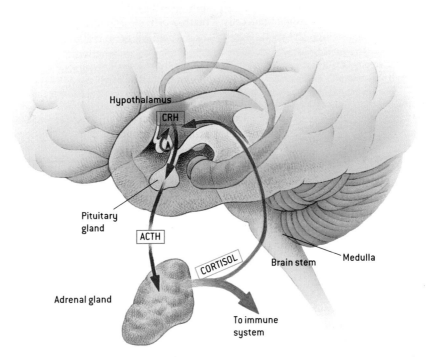

HPA AXIS—the interplay among the hypothalamus, the pituitary and the adrenal glands—is a central component of the brain's neuroendocrine response to stress. The hypothalamus, when stimulated, secretes corticotropin-releasing hormone (CRH) into the hypophyseal portal system, which supplies blood to the anterior pituitary. CRH stimulates the pituitary (*red arrows show stimulatory pathways*) to secrete adrenocorticotropin hormone (ACTH) into the bloodstream. ACTH causes the adrenal glands to release cortisol, the classic stress hormone that arouses the body to meet a challenging situation. But cortisol then modulates the stress response (*blue arrows indicate inhibitory effects*) by acting on the hypothalamus to inhibit the continued release of CRH. Also a potent immunoregulator, cortisol acts on many parts of the immune system to prevent it from overreacting and harming healthy cells and tissue.

In the past, the association between an inflammatory disease and stress was considered by doctors to be secondary to the chronic pain and debilitation of the disease. The recent discovery of the common underpinning of the immune and stress responses may provide an explanation of why a patient can be susceptible to both inflammatory disease and depression. The hormonal dysregulation that underlies both inflammatory disease and depression can lead to either illness, depending on whether the perturbing stimulus is pro-inflammatory or psychologically stressful. That may explain why the wax-

dividual's susceptibility to infectious diseases. The regulation of the immune system by the neurohormonal stress system provides a biological basis for understanding how stress might affect these diseases. Thus, stress hormones released from the brain, cortisol from the adrenal glands, and nerve chemicals released from nerve endings (adrenalinlike molecules norepinephrine and epinephrine) all modify the ability of immune cells to fight infectious agents and foreign molecules.

There is evidence that stress does affect human immune responses to viruses and bacteria. In studies with volunteers

es, such as herpes and influenza virus.

Animal studies provide further evidence that stress affects the course and severity of viral illness, bacterial disease and septic shock. Stress in mice worsens the severity of influenza infection through both the HPA axis and the sympathetic nervous system. Animal studies suggest that neuroendocrine mechanisms could play a similar role in infections with other viruses, including HIV, and provide a mechanism for understanding clinical observations that stress may exacerbate the course of AIDS. Stress, through cortisol, increases the susceptibility of mice to in-

Psychological STRESS CAN AFFECT an individual's SUSCEPTIBILITY to infectious diseases.

ing and waning of depression in arthritic patients does not always coincide with inflammatory flare-ups.

The popular belief that stress exacerbates inflammatory illness and that relaxation or removal of stress ameliorates it may indeed have a basis in fact. The interactions of the stress and immune systems and the hormonal responses they have in common could explain how conscious attempts to tone down responsivity to stress could affect immune responses.

Genetic Factors

HOW MUCH of the responsivity to stress is genetically determined and how much can be consciously controlled is not known. The set point of the stress response is to some extent genetically determined. In addition, factors in early development, learning, and later experiences contribute to differences in stress responsiveness. An event that is physiologically highly stressful to one individual may be much less so to another, depending on the sum of each person's genetic tendency to hormonal reactivity and their previous experience. The degree to which stress could precipitate or exacerbate disease would then depend not only on the intensity and duration of the stressful stimulus but also on the person's learned perception of the event as stressful and on the set point of the stress system.

Psychological stress can affect an in-

given a standard dose of the common cold virus (rhinovirus), individuals who are simultaneously exposed to stress show more viral particles and produce more mucus than do nonstressed individuals. Medical students receiving hepatitis vaccination during their final exams do not develop full protection against hepatitis. These findings have important implications for public health. People who are vaccinated during periods of stress might be less likely to develop full antibody protection. Chronic stress also prolongs wound healing.

New research shows that at physiological concentrations and under certain conditions the stress hormone cortisol not only is immunosuppressive but also may enhance certain aspects of immune function. Furthermore, each part of the stress response—the brain-hormonal, the adrenalinlike nerve and the adrenal gland adrenalin—is regulated independently, depending on the nature of the stressful stimulus. This specific nature of the stress response explains how different kinds and patterns of stress affect illness differently. Therefore, whereas chronic stress is generally immunosuppressive, acute stress can enhance cell-mediated immunity and exacerbate contact dermatitis types of allergic skin reactions. Furthermore, animal studies show that social stress and physical stress have different effects on infection with different virus-

fection with mycobacteria, the bacteria that causes tuberculosis. It has been shown that an intact HPA axis protects rats against the lethal septic effects of salmonella bacteria. Finally, new understanding of interactions of the immune and stress responses can help explain the puzzling observation that classic psychological conditioning of animals can influence their immune responses. For example, working with mice and rats, Robert Ader and Nicholas Cohen of the University of Rochester paired saccharin-flavored water with an immunosuppressive drug. Eventually the saccharin alone produced a decrease in immune function similar to that of the drug.

Social Stresses

STRESS NOT ONLY IS personal but is perceived through the prism of social interactions. These interactions can either add to or lessen psychological stress and affect our hormonal responses to it, which in turn can alter immune responses. Thus, the social-psychological stresses that we experience can affect our susceptibility to inflammatory and infectious diseases as well as the course of these and other diseases. For instance, in humans, loneliness is associated with a "threat," or adrenalinlike pattern of activation of the stress response and high blood pressure, whereas exercising is associated with a "challenge" pattern of high blood

IMMUNE SIGNALS TO THE BRAIN via the bloodstream can occur directly or indirectly. Immune cells such as monocytes, a type of white blood cell, produce a chemical messenger called interleukin-1 (IL-1), which ordinarily will not pass through the blood-brain barrier. But certain cerebral blood vessels contain leaky junctions, which allow IL-1 molecules to pass into the brain. There they can activate the HPA axis and other neural systems. IL-1 also binds to receptors on the endothelial cells that line cerebral blood vessels. This binding can cause enzymes in the cells to produce nitric oxide or prostaglandins, which diffuse into the brain and act directly on neurons.

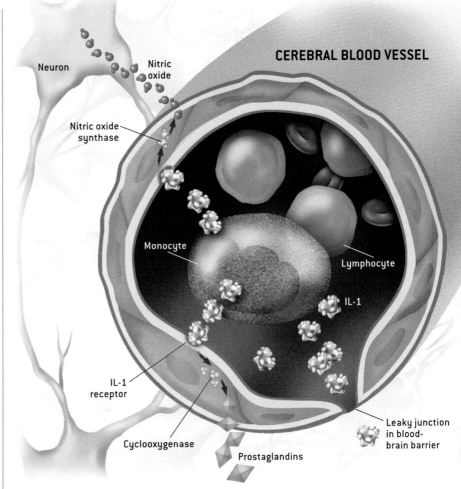

Neuron · Nitric oxide · Nitric oxide synthase · Monocyte · Lymphocyte · IL-1 · IL-1 receptor · Cyclooxygenase · Prostaglandins · Leaky junction in blood-brain barrier · CEREBRAL BLOOD VESSEL

flow and cardiac output. Studies have shown that people exposed to chronic social stresses for more than two months have increased susceptibility to the common cold.

Other studies have shown that the immune responses of long-term caregivers, such as spouses of Alzheimer's patients, become blunted. Immune responses during marital discord are also blunted in the spouse (usually the wife) who experiences the greatest amount of stress and feelings of helplessness. In such a scenario, studies have found that the levels of stress hormones are elevated in the affected spouse.

On the other hand, a positive supportive environment of extensive social networks or group psychotherapy can enhance immune response and resistance to disease—even cancer. Some studies have shown that women with breast cancer, for instance, who receive strong, positive social support during their illness have significantly longer life spans than women without such support.

For centuries, taking the cure at a mountain sanatorium or a hot-springs spa was the only available treatment for many chronic diseases. New understanding of the communication between the brain and immune system provides a physiological explanation of why such cures sometimes worked. Disruption of this communication network leads to an increase in susceptibility to disease and can worsen the course of the illness. Restoration of this communication system, whether through pharmacological agents or the relaxing effects of a spa, can be the first step on the road to recovery.

A corollary of these findings is that psychoactive drugs may be used to treat some inflammatory diseases, and drugs that affect the immune system may be useful in treating some psychiatric disorders. There is growing evidence that our view of ourselves and others, our style of handling stresses, and our genetic makeup can affect the immune system. Similarly, there is good evidence that diseases associated with chronic inflammation significantly affect one's mood or level of anxiety. Finally, these findings suggest that classification of illnesses into medical and psychiatric specialties, and the boundaries that have demarcated mind and body, are artificial. **SA**

MORE TO EXPLORE

Measuring Stress: A Guide for Health and Social Scientists. Edited by Sheldon Cohen, Ronald C. Kessler and Lynn Underwood Gordon. Oxford University Press, 1998.

Why Zebras Don't Get Ulcers: An Updated Guide to Stress-Related Disease and Coping. Robert M. Sapolsky. W. H. Freeman and Company, 1998.

The Cell Biology of the Blood-Brain Barrier. L. L. Rubin and J. M. Staddon in *Annual Review of Neuroscience*, Vol. 22, pages 11–28; 1999.

The Biological Basis for Mind Body Interactions. Edited by E. A. Mayer and C. B. Saper. *Progress in Brain Research*, Vol. 122. Elsevier Science, 2000.

The Autonomic Nervous System in Health and Disease. David S. Goldstein. Marcel Dekker, 2001.

The Balance Within: The Science Connecting Health and Emotions. Esther M. Sternberg. Henry Holt and Company, 2000 (paperbound, 2001).

Science of Mind-Body: An Exploration of Integrative Mechanisms. Videocast of conference, National Institutes of Health, March 26–28, 2001. The videocast can be found online at **http://videocast.nih.gov/PastEvents.asp?c+1&s+51**

Neuroendocrine Regulation of Immunity. Jeanette I. Webster, Leonardo Tonelli and Esther M. Sternberg in *Annual Review of Immunology*, Vol. 20, pages 125–163; 2002.

Neural Immune Interactions in Health and Disease. Esther M. Sternberg and J. I. Webster in *Fundamental Immunology*. Fifth edition. Edited by William E. Paul. Lippincott Williams & Wilkins (forthcoming).

LAURIE GRACE

Neuroscientists are finding that their biological descriptions of the brain may fit together best when integrated by psychological theories Freud sketched a century ago

Freud Returns

By Mark Solms

YOUNG FREUD,
circa 1891

FOR THE FIRST HALF OF THE 1900S,

the ideas of Sigmund Freud dominated explanations of how the human mind works. His basic proposition was that our motivations remain largely hidden in our unconscious minds. Moreover, they are actively withheld from consciousness by a repressive force. The executive apparatus of the mind (the ego) rejects any unconscious drives (the id) that might prompt behavior that would be incompatible with our civilized conception of ourselves. This repression is necessary because the drives express themselves in unconstrained passions, childish fantasies, and sexual and aggressive urges.

Mental illness, Freud said until his death in 1939, results when repression fails. Phobias, panic attacks and obsessions are caused by intrusions of the hidden drives into voluntary behavior. The aim of psychotherapy, then, was to trace neurotic symptoms back to their unconscious roots and expose these roots to mature, rational judgment, thereby depriving them of their compulsive power.

As mind and brain research grew more sophisticated from the 1950s onward, however, it became apparent to specialists that the evidence Freud had provided for his theories was rather tenuous. His principal method of investigation was not controlled experimentation but simple observations of patients in clinical settings, interwoven with theoretical inferences. Drug treatments gained ground, and biological approaches to mental illness gradually overshadowed psychoanalysis. Had Freud lived, he might even have welcomed this turn of events. A highly regarded neuroscientist in his day, he frequently made remarks such as "the deficiencies in our description would presumably vanish if we were already in a position to replace the psychological terms by physiological and chemical ones." But Freud did not have the science or technology to know how the brain of a normal or neurotic personality was organized.

By the 1980s the notions of ego and id were considered hopelessly antiquated, even in some psychoanalytical circles. Freud was history. In the new psychology, the updated thinking went, depressed people do not feel so wretched because something has undermined their earliest attachments in infancy—rather their brain chemicals are unbalanced. Psychopharmacology, however, did not deliver an alternative grand theory of personality, emotion and motivation—a new conception of "what makes us tick." Without this model, neuroscientists focused their work narrowly and left the big picture alone.

Today that picture is coming back into focus, and the surprise is this: it is not unlike the one that Freud outlined a century ago. We are still far from a consensus, but an increasing number of diverse neuroscientists are reaching the same conclusion drawn by Eric R. Kandel of Columbia University, the 2000 Nobel laureate in physiology or medicine: that psychoanalysis is "still the most coherent and intellectually satisfying view of the mind."

Freud is back, and not just in theory. Interdisciplinary work groups uniting the previously divided and often antagonistic fields of neuroscience and psychoanalysis have been formed in almost every major city of the world. These networks, in turn, have come together as the International Neuro-Psychoanalysis Society, which organizes an annual congress and publishes the successful journal *Neuro-Psychoanalysis*. Testament to the renewed respect for Freud's ideas is the journal's editorial advisory board, populated by a who's who of experts in contemporary behavioral neuroscience, including Antonio R. Damasio, Kandel, Joseph E. LeDoux, Benjamin Libet, Jaak Panksepp, Vilayanur S. Ramachandran, Daniel L. Schacter and Wolf Singer.

Together these researchers are forging what Kandel calls a "new intellectual framework for psychiatry." Within this framework, it appears that Freud's broad brushstroke organization of the mind is destined to play a role similar to the one Darwin's theory of evolution

Overview/*Mind Models*

- For decades, Freudian concepts such as ego, id and repressed desires dominated psychology and psychiatry's attempts to cure mental illnesses. But better understanding of brain chemistry gradually replaced this model with a biological explanation of how the mind arises from neuronal activity.
- The latest attempts to piece together diverse neurological findings, however, are leading to a chemical framework of the mind that validates the general sketch Freud made almost a century ago. A growing group of scientists are eager to reconcile neurology and psychiatry into a unified theory.

served for molecular genetics—a template on which emerging details can be coherently arranged. At the same time, neuroscientists are uncovering proof for some of Freud's theories and are teasing out the mechanisms behind the mental processes he described.

Unconscious Motivation

WHEN FREUD INTRODUCED the central notion that most mental processes that determine our everyday thoughts, feelings and volitions occur unconsciously, his contemporaries rejected it as impossible. But today's findings are confirming the existence and pivotal role of unconscious mental processing. For example, the behavior of patients who are unable to consciously remember events that occurred after damage to certain memory-encoding structures of their brains is clearly influenced by the "forgotten" events. Cognitive neuroscientists make sense of such cases by delineating different memory systems that process information "explicitly" (consciously) and "implicitly" (unconsciously). Freud split memory along just these lines.

Neuroscientists have also identified unconscious memory systems that mediate emotional learning. In 1996 at New York University, LeDoux demonstrated the existence under the conscious cortex of a neuronal pathway that connects perceptual information with the primitive brain structures responsible for generating fear responses. Because this pathway bypasses the hippocampus—which generates conscious memories—current events routinely trigger unconscious remembrances of emotionally important past events, causing conscious feelings that seem irrational, such as "Men with beards make me uneasy."

Neuroscience has shown that the major brain structures essential for forming conscious (explicit) memories are not functional during the first two years of life, providing an elegant explanation of what Freud called infantile amnesia. As Freud surmised, it is not that we forget our earliest memories; we simply cannot recall them to consciousness. But this inability does not preclude them from affecting adult feelings and behavior. One would be hard-pressed to find a developmental neurobiologist who does not agree that early experiences, especially between mother and infant, influence the pattern of brain connections in ways that fundamentally shape our future personality and mental health. Yet none of these experiences can be consciously remembered. It is becoming increasingly clear that a good deal of our mental activity is unconsciously motivated.

Repression Vindicated

EVEN IF WE ARE MOSTLY driven by unconscious thoughts, this does not prove anything about Freud's claim that we actively repress unpalatable information. But case studies supporting that notion are beginning to accumulate. The most famous one comes from a 1994 study of "anosognosic" patients by behavioral neurologist Ramachandran of the University of California at San Diego. Damage to the right parietal region of these people's brains makes them unaware of gross physical defects, such as paralysis of a limb. After artificially activating the right hemisphere of one such patient, Ramachandran observed that she suddenly became aware that her left arm was paralyzed—and that it had been paralyzed continuously since she had suffered a stroke eight days before. This showed that she was capable of recog-

MIND AND MATTER

Freud drew his final model of the mind in 1933 (*right; color has been added*). Dotted lines represented the threshold between unconscious and conscious processing. The superego repressed instinctual drives (the id), preventing them from disrupting rational thought. Most rational (ego) processes were automatic and unconscious, too, so only a small part of the ego (*bulb at top*) was left to manage conscious experience, which was closely tied to perception. The superego mediated the ongoing struggle between the ego and id for dominance. Recent neurological mapping (*below*) generally correlates to Freud's conception. The core brain stem and limbic system—responsible for instincts and drives—roughly correspond to Freud's id. The ventral frontal region, which controls selective inhibition, the dorsal frontal region, which controls self-conscious thought, and the posterior cortex, which represents the outside world, amount to the ego and the superego.

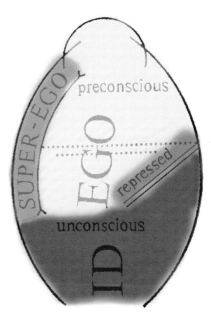

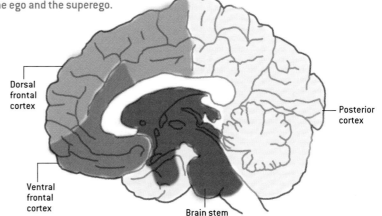

Dorsal frontal cortex

Ventral frontal cortex

Brain stem

Posterior cortex

A. W. FREUD ET AL., BY ARRANGEMENT WITH PATERSON MARSH LTD., LONDON (*top*); OLIVER TURNBULL (*bottom; all coloring*)

nizing her deficits and that she had unconsciously registered these deficits for the previous eight days, despite her conscious denials during that time that there was any problem.

Significantly, after the effects of the stimulation wore off, the woman not only reverted to the belief that her arm was normal, she also forgot the part of the interview in which she had acknowledged that the arm was paralyzed, even though she remembered every other detail about

Like "split-brain" patients, whose hemispheres become unlinked—made famous in studies by the late Nobel laureate Roger W. Sperry of the California Institute of Technology in the 1960s and 1970s—anosognosic patients typically rationalize away unwelcome facts, giving plausible but invented explanations of their unconsciously motivated actions. In this way, Ramachandran says, the left hemisphere manifestly employs Freudian "mechanisms of defense."

Durham neuropsychologist Aikaterini Fotopoulou recently studied a patient of this type in my laboratory. The man failed to recall, in each 50-minute session held in my office on 12 consecutive days, that he had ever met me before or that he had undergone an operation to remove a tumor in his frontal lobes that caused his amnesia. As far as he was concerned, there was nothing wrong with him. When asked about the scar on his head, he confabulated wholly implausible explana-

Freud himself anticipated the day
when neurological data
would round out his psychological ideas.

the interview. Ramachandran concluded: "The remarkable theoretical implication of these observations is that memories can indeed be selectively repressed.... Seeing [this patient] convinced me, for the first time, of the reality of the repression phenomena that form the cornerstone of classical psychoanalytical theory."

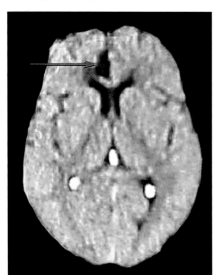

BRAIN SCANS show the damage that causes disorders of psychological function, which Freud could study only clinically. A recent MRI image of a patient who confabulates grandiose stories of his life reveals a lesion (*arrow*) in the cingulate gyrus—part of the medial frontal lobe that serves functions Freud posited would normally prevent unconscious wishes from altering a person's rational self-image.

Analogous phenomena have now been demonstrated in people with intact brains, too. As neuropsychologist Martin A. Conway of Durham University in England pointed out in a 2001 commentary in *Nature*, if significant repression effects can be generated in average people in an innocuous laboratory setting, then far greater effects are likely in real-life traumatic situations.

The Pleasure Principle

FREUD WENT EVEN further, though. He said that not only is much of our mental life unconscious and withheld but that the repressed part of the unconscious mind operates according to a different principle than the "reality principle" that governs the conscious ego. This type of unconscious thinking is "wishful"—and it blithely disregards the rules of logic and the arrow of time.

If Freud was right, then damage to the inhibitory structures of the brain (the seat of the "repressing" ego) should release wishful, irrational modes of mental functioning. This is precisely what has been observed in patients with damage to the frontal limbic region, which controls critical aspects of self-awareness. Subjects display a striking syndrome known as Korsakoff's psychosis: they are unaware that they are amnesic and therefore fill the gaps in their memory with fabricated stories known as confabulations.

tions: he had undergone dental surgery or a coronary bypass operation. In reality, he had indeed experienced these procedures—years before—and unlike his brain operation, they had successful outcomes.

Similarly, when asked who I was and what he was doing in my lab, he variously said that I was a colleague, a drinking partner, a client consulting him about his area of professional expertise, a teammate in a sport that he had not participated in since he was in college decades earlier, or a mechanic repairing one of his numerous sports cars (which he did not possess). His behavior was consistent with these false beliefs, too: he would look around the room for his beer or out the window for his car.

What strikes the casual observer is the wishful quality of these false notions, an impression that Fotopoulou confirmed objectively through quantitative analysis of a consecutive series of 155 of his confabulations. The patient's false beliefs were not random noise—they were generated by the "pleasure principle" that Freud maintained was central to unconscious thought. The man simply recast reality as he wanted it to be. Similar observations have been reported by others, such as Martin Conway of Durham and Oliver Turnbull of the University of Wales. These investigators are cognitive neuroscientists, not psychoanalysts, yet they interpret their findings in Freudian terms, claiming in essence that damage to the frontal limbic region that produces confabulations impairs cognitive control mechanisms that underpin normal reality monitoring and releases from inhibition the implicit wishful influences on perception, memory and judgment.

Animal Within

FREUD ARGUED THAT the pleasure principle gave expression to primitive, animal drives. To his Victorian contemporaries, the implication that human behavior was at bottom governed by urges that served no higher purpose than carnal self-fulfillment was downright scandalous. The moral outrage waned during subsequent decades, but Freud's concept of man-as-animal was pretty much sidelined by cognitive scientists.

Now it has returned. Neuroscientists such as Donald W. Pfaff of the Rockefeller University and Jaak Panksepp of Bowling Green State University believe that the instinctual mechanisms that govern human motivation are even more primitive than Freud imagined. We share basic emotional-control systems with our primate relatives and with all mammals. At the deep level of mental organization that Freud called the id, the functional anatomy and chemistry of our brains is not much different from that of our favorite barnyard animals and household pets.

Modern neuroscientists do not accept Freud's classification of human instinctual life as a simple dichotomy between sexuality and aggression, however. Instead, through studies of lesions and the effects of drugs and artificial stimulation on the brain, they have identified at least four basic mammalian instinctual circuits, some of which overlap. They are the "seeking" or "reward" system (which motivates the pursuit of pleasure); the "anger-rage" system (which governs angry aggression but not predatory aggression); the "fear-anxiety" system; and the "panic" system (which includes complex instincts such as those that govern social bonding). Whether other instinctual forces exist, such as a rough-and-tumble "play" system, is also being investigated. All these brain sys-

FREUD SKETCHED a neuronal mechanism for repression (*above*) in 1895, as part of his hope that biological explanations of the mind would one day replace psychological ones. In his scheme, an unpleasant memory would normally be activated by a stimulus (*"Qn," far left*) heading from neuron "a" toward neuron "b" (*bottom*). But neuron "alpha" (*to right of "a"*) could divert the signal and thus prevent the activation if other neurons (*top right*) exerted a "repressing" influence. Note that Freud (*shown later in life*) drew gaps between neurons that he predicted would act as "contact barriers." Two years later English physiologist Charles Sherrington discovered such gaps and named them synapses.

tems are modulated by specific neurotransmitters, chemicals that carry messages between the brain's neurons.

The seeking system, regulated by the neurotransmitter dopamine, bears a remarkable resemblance to the Freudian "libido." According to Freud, the libidinal or sexual drive is a pleasure-seeking system that energizes most of our goal-directed interactions with the world. Modern research shows that its neural equivalent is heavily implicated in almost all forms of craving and addiction. It is interesting to note that Freud's early experiments with cocaine—mainly on himself—convinced him that the libido must have a specific neurochemical foundation. Unlike his successors, Freud saw no reason for antagonism between psychoanalysis and psychopharmacology. He enthusiastically anticipated the day when

"id energies" would be controlled directly by "particular chemical substances." Today treatments that integrate psychotherapy with psychoactive medications are widely recognized as the best approach for many disorders. And brain imaging shows that talk therapy affects the brain in similar ways to such drugs.

Dreams Have Meaning

FREUD'S IDEAS ARE also reawakening in sleep and dream science. His dream theory—that nighttime visions are partial glimpses of unconscious wishes—was discredited when rapid-eye-movement (REM) sleep and its strong correlation with dreaming were discovered in the 1950s. Freud's view appeared to lose all credibility when investigators in the 1970s showed that the dream cycle was regulated by the pervasive brain chemi-

THE AUTHOR

MARK SOLMS holds the chair in neuropsychology at the University of Cape Town in South Africa and an honorary lectureship in neurosurgery at St. Bartholomew's and the Royal London School of Medicine and Dentistry. He is also director of the Arnold Pfeffer Center for Neuro-Psychoanalysis of the New York Psychoanalytic Institute, a consultant neuropsychologist to the Anna Freud Center in London and a very frequent flier. Solms is editor and translator of the forthcoming four-volume series *The Complete Neuroscientific Works of Sigmund Freud* (Karnac Books). Solms thanks Oliver Turnbull, a senior lecturer at the University of Wales Center for Cognitive Neuroscience in Bangor, for assisting with this article.

cal acetylcholine, produced in a "mindless" part of the brain stem. REM sleep occurred automatically, every 90 minutes or so, and was driven by brain chemicals and structures that had nothing to do with emotion or motivation. This discovery implied that dreams had no meaning; they were simply stories concocted by the higher brain to try to reflect the random cortical activity caused by REM.

But more recent work has revealed

with impunity—that dream content has no primary emotional mechanism.

Finishing the Job

NOT EVERYONE IS enthusiastic about the reappearance of Freudian concepts in the mainstream of mental science. It is not easy for the older generation of psychoanalysts, for example, to accept that their junior colleagues and students now can and must subject conventional wisdom to

zine, for neuroscientists who are enthusiastic about the reconciliation of neurology and psychiatry, "it is not a matter of proving Freud right or wrong, but of finishing the job."

If that job can be finished—if Kandel's "new intellectual framework for psychiatry" can be established—then the time will pass when people with emotional difficulties have to choose between the talk therapy of psychoanalysis, which

If scientists can reconcile neurology and psychology, then patients could receive more integrated treatment.

that dreaming and REM sleep are dissociable states, controlled by distinct, though interactive, mechanisms. Dreaming turns out to be generated by a network of structures centered on the forebrain's instinctual-motivational circuitry. This discovery has given rise to a host of theories about the dreaming brain, many strongly reminiscent of Freud's. Most intriguing is the observation that others and I have made that dreaming stops completely when certain fibers deep in the frontal lobe have been severed—a symptom that coincides with a general reduction in motivated behavior. The lesion is exactly the same as the damage that was deliberately produced in prefrontal leukotomy, an outmoded surgical procedure that was once used to control hallucinations and delusions. This operation was replaced in the 1960s by drugs that dampen dopamine's activity in the same brain systems. The seeking system, then, might be the primary generator of dreams. This possibility has become a major focus of current research.

If the hypothesis is confirmed, then the wish-fulfillment theory of dreams could once again set the agenda for sleep research. But even if other interpretations of the new neurological data prevail, all of them demonstrate that "psychological" conceptualizations of dreaming are scientifically respectable again. Few neuroscientists still claim—as they once did

an entirely new level of biological scrutiny. But an encouraging number of elders on both sides of the Atlantic are at least committed to keeping an open mind, as evidenced by the aforementioned eminent psychoanalysts on the advisory board of *Neuro-Psychoanalysis* and by the many graying participants in the International Neuro-Psychoanalysis Society.

For older neuroscientists, resistance to the return of psychoanalytical ideas comes from the specter of the seemingly indestructible edifice of Freudian theory in the early years of their careers. They cannot acknowledge even partial confirmation of Freud's fundamental insights; they demand a complete purge [*see box on opposite page*]. In the words of J. Allan Hobson, a renowned sleep researcher and Harvard Medical School psychiatrist, the renewed interest in Freud is little more than unhelpful "retrofitting" of modern data into an antiquated theoretical framework. But as Panksepp said in a 2002 interview with *Newsweek* magazine.

may be out of touch with modern evidence-based medicine, and the drugs prescribed by psychopharmacology, which may lack regard for the relation between the brain chemistries it manipulates and the complex real-life trajectories that culminate in emotional distress. The psychiatry of tomorrow promises to provide patients with help that is grounded in a deeply integrated understanding of how the human mind operates.

Whatever undreamed-of therapies the future might bring, patients can only benefit from better knowledge of how the brain really works. As modern neuroscientists tackle once more the profound questions of human psychology that so preoccupied Freud, it is gratifying to find that we can build on the foundations he laid, instead of having to start all over again. Even as we identify the weak points in Freud's far-reaching theories, and thereby correct, revise and supplement his work, we are excited to have the privilege of finishing the job.　　SA

MORE TO EXPLORE

The Neuropsychology of Dreams. Mark Solms. Lawrence Erlbaum Associates, 1997.

Dreaming and REM Sleep Are Controlled by Different Brain Mechanisms. Mark Solms in *Behavioral and Brain Sciences*, Vol. 23, No. 6, pages 843–850; December 2000.

Freudian Dream Theory Today. Mark Solms in *Psychologist*, Vol. 13, No. 12, pages 618–619; December 2000.

Clinical Studies in Neuro-Psychoanalysis. K. Kaplan-Solms and M. Solms. Karnac Books, 2000.

The Brain and the Inner World. Mark Solms and Oliver Turnbull. Other Press, 2002.

The International Neuro-Psychoanalysis Society and the journal *Neuro-Psychoanalysis*: www.neuro-psa.org

FREUD RETURNS? LIKE A BAD DREAM

By J. Allan Hobson

Sigmund Freud's views on the meaning of dreams formed the core of his theory of mental functioning. Mark Solms and others assert that brain imaging and lesion studies are now validating Freud's conception of the mind. But similar scientific investigations show that major aspects of Freud's thinking are probably erroneous.

For Freud, the bizarre nature of dreams resulted from an elaborate effort of the mind to conceal, by symbolic disguise and censorship, the unacceptable instinctual wishes welling up from the unconscious when the ego relaxes its prohibition of the id in sleep. But most neurobiological evidence supports the alternative view that dream bizarreness stems from normal changes in brain state. Chemical mechanisms in the brain stem, which shift the activation of various regions of the cortex, generate these changes. Many studies have indicated that the chemical changes determine the quality and quantity of dream visions, emotions and thoughts. Freud's disguise-and-censorship notion must be discarded; no one believes that the ego-id struggle, if it exists, controls brain chemistry. Most psychoanalysts no longer hold that the disguise-censorship theory is valid.

Without disguise and censorship, what is left of Freud's dream theory? Not much—only that instinctual drives could impel dream formation. Evidence does indicate that activating the parts of the limbic system that produce anxiety, anger and elation shapes dreams. But these influences are not "wishes." Dream analyses show that the emotions in dreams are as often negative as they are positive, which would mean that half our "wishes" for ourselves are negative. And as all dreamers know, the emotions in dreams are hardly disguised. They enter into dream plots clearly, frequently bringing unpleasant effects such as nightmares. Freud was never able to account for why so many dream emotions are negative.

Another pillar of Freud's model is that because the true meaning of dreams is hidden, the emotions they reflect can be revealed only through his wild-goose-

chase method of free association, in which the subject relates anything and everything that comes to mind in hopes of stumbling across a crucial connection. But this effort is unnecessary, because no such concealment occurs. In dreams,

what you see is what you get. Dream content is emotionally salient on its face, and the close attention of dreamers and their therapists is all that is needed to see the feelings they represent.

Solms and other Freudians intimate that ascribing dreams to brain chemistry is the same as saying that dreams have no emotional messages. But the statements are not equivalent. The chemical activation-synthesis theory of dreaming, put forth by Robert W. McCarley of Harvard Medical School and me in 1977, maintained only that the psychoanalytic explanation of dream bizarreness as concealed meaning was wrong. We have always argued that dreams are emotionally salient and meaningful. And what about REM sleep? New studies reveal that dreams can occur

during non-REM sleep, but nothing in the chemical activation model precludes this case; the frequency of dreams is simply exponentially higher during REM sleep.

Psychoanalysis is in big trouble, and no amount of neurobiological tinkering can fix it. So radical an overhaul is necessary that many neuroscientists would prefer to start over and create a neurocognitive model of the mind. Psychoanalytic theory is indeed comprehensive, but if it is terribly in error, then its comprehensiveness is hardly a virtue. The scientists who share this view stump for more biologically based models of dreams, of mental illness, and of normal conscious experience than those offered by psychoanalysis.

J. Allan Hobson, professor of psychiatry at Harvard Medical School, has written extensively on the brain basis of the mind and its implications for psychiatry. For more, see Hobson's book Dreaming: An Introduction to the Science of Sleep *(Oxford University Press, 2003).*

Manic-Depressive Illness and Creativity

Does some fine madness plague great artists?
Several studies now show that creativity
and mood disorders are linked

by Kay Redfield Jamison

The Author

KAY REDFIELD JAMISON is professor of psychiatry at the Johns Hopkins University School of Medicine. She wrote *Touched with Fire: Manic-Depressive Illness and the Artistic Temperament* and co-authored the medical text *Manic-Depressive Illness.* Jamison is a member of the National Advisory Council for Human Genome Research and clinical director of the Dana Consortium on the Genetic Basis of Manic-Depressive Illness. She has also written and produced a series of public television specials about manic-depressive illness and the arts.

"M en have called me mad," wrote Edgar Allan Poe, "but the question is not yet settled, whether madness is or is not the loftiest intelligence—whether much that is glorious—whether all that is profound—does not spring from disease of thought—from moods of mind exalted at the expense of the general intellect."

Many people have long shared Poe's suspicion that genius and insanity are entwined. Indeed, history holds countless examples of "that fine madness." Scores of influential 18th- and 19th-century poets, notably William Blake, Lord Byron and Alfred, Lord Tennyson, wrote about the extreme mood swings they endured. Modern American poets John Berryman, Randall Jarrell, Robert Lowell, Sylvia Plath, Theodore Roethke, Delmore Schwartz and Anne Sexton were all hospitalized for either mania or depression during their lives. And many painters and composers, among them Vincent van Gogh, Georgia O'Keeffe, Charles Mingus and Robert Schumann, have been similarly afflicted.

Judging by current diagnostic criteria, it seems that most of these artists—and many others besides—suffered from one of the major mood disorders, namely, manic-depressive illness or major depression. Both are fairly common, very treatable and yet frequently lethal diseases. Major depression induces intense melancholic spells, whereas manic-depression,

Van Gogh painted flowers while in the asylum at Saint-Rémy.

Vincent van Gogh

Tennessee Williams

AP/WIDE WORLD PHOTOS

Reprinted from the February 1995 issue

Anne Sexton

Ezra Pound

a strongly genetic disease, pitches patients repeatedly from depressed to hyperactive and euphoric, or intensely irritable, states. In its milder form, termed cyclothymia, manic-depression causes pronounced but not totally debilitating changes in mood, behavior, sleep, thought patterns and energy levels. Advanced cases are marked by dramatic, cyclic shifts.

Could such disruptive diseases convey certain creative advantages? Many people find that proposition counterin-tuitive. Most manic-depressives do not possess extraordinary imagination, and most accomplished artists do not suffer from recurring mood swings. To assume, then, that such diseases usually promote artistic talent wrongly reinforces simplistic notions of the "mad genius." Worse yet, such a generalization trivializes a very serious medical condition and, to some degree, discredits individuality in the arts as well. It would be wrong to label anyone who is unusually accomplished, energetic, intense, moody or eccentric as manic-depressive. All the same, recent studies indicate that a high number of established artists—far more than could be expected by chance— meet the diagnostic criteria for manic-depression or major depression given in the fourth edition of the *Diagnostic and Statistical Manual of Mental Disorders* (*DSM-IV*). In fact, it seems that these diseases can sometimes enhance or otherwise contribute to creativity in some people.

By virtue of their prevalence alone, it is clear that mood disorders do not necessarily breed genius. Indeed, 1 percent of the general population suffer from manic-depression, also called bipolar disorder, and 5 percent from a major depression, or unipolar disorder, during their lifetime. Depression affects twice as many women as men and most often, but not always, strikes later in life. Bipolar disorder afflicts equal numbers of women and men, and more than a third of all cases surface before age 20. Some 60 to 80 percent of all adoles-

Charles Mingus

ARTISTS, writers and composers shown on these pages all most likely suffered from manic-depressive illness or major depressive illness, according to their letters and journals, medical records and accounts by their families and friends. Recent studies indicate that the temperaments and cognitive styles associated with mood disorders can in fact enhance creativity in some individuals.

The Tainted Blood of the Tennysons

Alfred, Lord Tennyson (*right*), who experienced recurrent, debilitating depressions and probable hypomanic spells, often expressed fear that he might inherit the madness, or "taint of blood," in his family. His father, grandfather, two of his great-grandfathers as well as five of his seven brothers suffered from insanity, melancholia, uncontrollable rage or what is today known as manic-depressive illness. His brother Edward was confined to an asylum for nearly 60 years before he died from manic exhaustion. Lionel Tennyson, one of Alfred's two sons, displayed a mercurial temperament, as did one of his three grandsons.

Modern medicine has confirmed that manic-depression and creativity tend to run in certain families. Studies of twins provide strong evidence for the heritability of manic-depressive illness. If an identical twin has manic-depressive illness, the other twin typically has a 70 to 100 percent chance of also having the disease; if the other twin is fraternal, the chances are considerably lower (approximately 20 percent). A review of pairs of identical twins reared apart from birth—in which at least one had been diagnosed as manic-depressive—found that in two thirds or more of the sets, the illness was present in both twins. —*K. R. J.*

CORBIS-BETTMANN

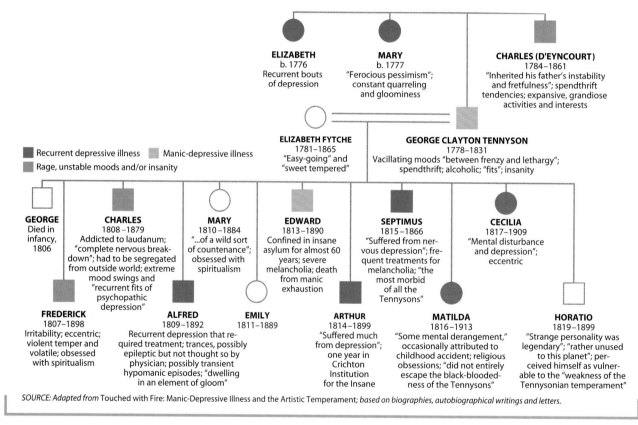

Legend:
- Recurrent depressive illness
- Manic-depressive illness
- Rage, unstable moods and/or insanity

ELIZABETH b. 1776 Recurrent bouts of depression

MARY b. 1777 "Ferocious pessimism"; constant quarreling and gloominess

CHARLES (D'EYNCOURT) 1784–1861 "Inherited his father's instability and fretfulness"; spendthrift tendencies; expansive, grandiose activities and interests

ELIZABETH FYTCHE 1781–1865 "Easy-going" and "sweet tempered"

GEORGE CLAYTON TENNYSON 1778–1831 Vacillating moods "between frenzy and lethargy"; spendthrift; alcoholic; "fits"; insanity

GEORGE Died in infancy, 1806

CHARLES 1808–1879 Addicted to laudanum; "complete nervous breakdown"; had to be segregated from outside world; extreme mood swings and "recurrent fits of psychopathic depression"

MARY 1810–1884 "...of a wild sort of countenance"; obsessed with spiritualism

EDWARD 1813–1890 Confined in insane asylum for almost 60 years; severe melancholia; death from manic exhaustion

SEPTIMUS 1815–1866 "Suffered from nervous depression"; frequent treatments for melancholia; "the most morbid of all the Tennysons"

CECILIA 1817–1909 "Mental disturbance and depression"; eccentric

FREDERICK 1807–1898 Irritability; eccentric; violent temper and volatile; obsessed with spiritualism

ALFRED 1809–1892 Recurrent depression that required treatment; trances, possibly epileptic but not thought so by physician; possibly transient hypomanic episodes; "dwelling in an element of gloom"

EMILY 1811–1889

ARTHUR 1814–1899 "Suffered much from depression"; one year in Crichton Institution for the Insane

MATILDA 1816–1913 "Some mental derangement," occasionally attributed to childhood accident; religious obsessions; "did not entirely escape the black-bloodedness of the Tennysons"

HORATIO 1819–1899 "Strange personality was legendary"; "rather unused to this planet"; perceived himself as vulnerable to the "weakness of the Tennysonian temperament"

LISA BURNETT

SOURCE: Adapted from Touched with Fire: Manic-Depressive Illness and the Artistic Temperament; *based on biographies, autobiographical writings and letters.*

---

cents and adults who commit suicide have a history of bipolar or unipolar illness. Before the late 1970s, when the drug lithium first became widely available, one person in five with manic-depression committed suicide.

Major depression in both unipolar and bipolar disorders manifests itself through apathy, lethargy, hopelessness, sleep disturbances, slowed physical movements and thinking, impaired memory and concentration, and a loss of pleasure in typically enjoyable events. The diagnostic criteria also include suicidal thinking, self-blame and inappropriate guilt. To distinguish clinical depression from normal periods of unhappiness, the common guidelines further require that these symptoms persist for a minimum of two to four weeks and also that they significantly interfere with a person's everyday functioning.

Mood Elevation

During episodes of mania or hypomania (mild mania), bipolar patients experience symptoms that are in many ways the opposite of those associated with depression. Their mood and self-esteem are elevated. They sleep less and have abundant energy; their productivity increases. Manics frequently become paranoid and irritable. Moreover, their speech is often rapid, excitable and intrusive, and their thoughts move quickly and fluidly from one topic to another. They usually hold tremendous conviction about the correctness and importance of their own ideas as well. This grandiosity can contribute to poor judgment and impulsive behavior.

Hypomanics and manics generally have chaotic personal and professional relationships. They may spend large sums of money, drive recklessly or pursue questionable business ventures or sexual liaisons. In some cases, manics suffer from violent agitation and delusional thoughts as well as visual and auditory hallucinations.

Rates of Mood Disorders

For years, scientists have documented some kind of connection between mania, depression and creative output. In the late 19th and early 20th centuries, researchers turned to accounts of mood disorders written by prominent artists, their physicians and friends. Although largely anecdotal, this work strongly suggested that renowned writers, artists and composers—and their first-degree relatives—were far more likely to experience mood disorders and to commit suicide than was the general population. During the past 20 years, more systematic studies of artistic populations have confirmed these findings [*see illustration below*]. Diagnostic and psychological analyses of living writers and artists can give quite meaningful estimates of the rates and types of psychopathology they experience.

In the 1970s Nancy C. Andreasen of the University of Iowa completed the first of these rigorous studies, which made use of structured interviews, matched control groups and strict diagnostic criteria. She examined 30 creative writers and found an extraordinarily high occurrence of mood disorders and alcoholism among them. Eighty percent had experienced at least one episode of major depression, hypomania or mania; 43 percent reported a history of hypomania or mania. Also, the relatives of these writers, compared with the relatives of the control subjects, generally performed more creative work and more often had a mood disorder.

A few years later, while on sabbatical in England from the University of California at Los Angeles, I began a study of 47 distinguished British writers and visual artists. To select the group as best I could for creativity, I purposefully chose painters and sculptors who were Royal Academicians or Associates of the Royal Academy. All the playwrights had won the New York Drama Critics Award or the Evening Standard Drama (London Critics) Award, or both. Half of the poets were already represented in the *Oxford Book of Twentieth Century English Verse*. I found that 38 percent of these artists and writers had in fact been previously treated for a mood disorder; three fourths of those treated had required medication or hospitalization, or both. And half of the poets—the largest fraction from any one group—had needed such extensive care.

Hagop S. Akiskal of the University of California at San Diego, also affiliated with the University of Tennessee at Memphis, and his wife, Kareen Akiskal, subsequently interviewed 20 award-winning European writers, poets, painters and sculptors. Some two thirds of their subjects exhibited recurrent cyclothymic or hypomanic tendencies, and half had at one time suffered from a major depression. In collaboration with David H. Evans of the University of Memphis, the Akiskals noted the same trends among living blues musicians. More recently Stuart A. Montgomery and his wife, Deirdre B. Montgomery, of St. Mary's Hospital in London examined 50 modern British poets. One fourth met current diagnostic criteria for depression or manic-depression; suicide was six times more frequent in this community than in the general population.

Ruth L. Richards and her colleagues at Harvard University set up a system for assessing the degree of original thinking required to perform certain creative tasks. Then, rather than screening for mood disorders among those already deemed highly inventive, they attempted to rate creativity in a sample of manic-depressive patients. Based on their scale, they found that compared with individuals having no personal or family history of psychiatric disorders, manic-depressive and cyclothymic patients (as well as their unaffected relatives) showed greater creativity.

Biographical studies of earlier generations of artists and writers also show consistently high rates of suicide, depression and manic-depression—up to 18 times the rate of suicide seen in the general population, eight to 10 times that of depression and 10 to 20 times that of manic-depressive illness and its milder variants. Joseph J. Schildkraut and his co-workers at Harvard concluded that approximately half of the 15 20th-cen-

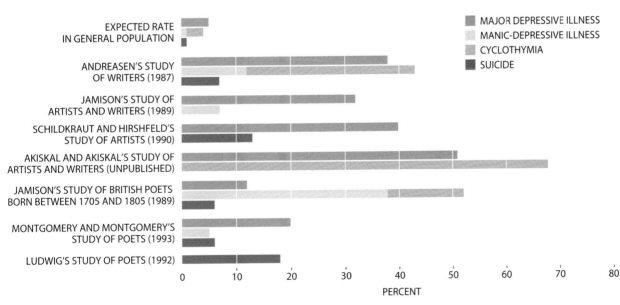

EXPECTED RATE IN GENERAL POPULATION

ANDREASEN'S STUDY OF WRITERS (1987)

JAMISON'S STUDY OF ARTISTS AND WRITERS (1989)

SCHILDKRAUT AND HIRSHFELD'S STUDY OF ARTISTS (1990)

AKISKAL AND AKISKAL'S STUDY OF ARTISTS AND WRITERS (UNPUBLISHED)

JAMISON'S STUDY OF BRITISH POETS BORN BETWEEN 1705 AND 1805 (1989)

MONTGOMERY AND MONTGOMERY'S STUDY OF POETS (1993)

LUDWIG'S STUDY OF POETS (1992)

■ MAJOR DEPRESSIVE ILLNESS
  MANIC-DEPRESSIVE ILLNESS
  CYCLOTHYMIA
■ SUICIDE

PERCENT

INCREASED RATES OF SUICIDE, depression and manic-depression among artists have been established by many separate studies. These investigations show that artists experience up to 18 times the rate of suicide seen in the general population, eight to 10 times the rate of depression and 10 to 20 times the rate of manic-depression and its milder form, cyclothymia.

tury abstract-expressionist artists they studied suffered from depressive or manic-depressive illness; the suicide rate in this group was at least 13 times the current U.S. national rate.

In 1992 Arnold M. Ludwig of the University of Kentucky published an extensive biographical survey of 1,005 famous 20th-century artists, writers and other professionals, some of whom had been in treatment for a mood disorder. He discovered that the artists and writers experienced two to three times the rate of psychosis, suicide attempts, mood disorders and substance abuse that comparably successful people in business, science and public life did. The poets in this sample had most often been manic or psychotic and hospitalized; they also proved to be some 18 times more likely to commit suicide than is the general public. In a comprehensive biographical study of 36 major British poets born between 1705 and 1805, I found similarly elevated rates of psychosis and severe psychopathology. These poets were 30 times more likely to have had manic-depressive illness than were their contemporaries, at least 20 times more likely to have been committed to an asylum and some five times more likely to have taken their own life.

These corroborative studies have confirmed that highly creative individuals experience major mood disorders more often than do other groups in the general population. But what does this mean for their work? How does a psychiatric illness contribute to creative achievement? First, the common features of hypomania seem highly conducive to original thinking; the diagnostic criteria for this phase of the disorder include "sharpened and unusually creative thinking and increased productivity." And accumulating evidence suggests that the cognitive styles associated with hypomania (expansive thought and grandiose moods) can lead to increased fluency and frequency of thoughts.

Mania and Creativity

Studying the speech of hypomanic patients has revealed that they tend to rhyme and use other sound associations, such as alliteration, far more often than do unaffected individuals. They also use idiosyncratic words nearly three times as often as do control subjects. Moreover, in specific drills, they can list synonyms or form other word associations much more rapidly than is considered normal. It seems, then, that both the quantity and quality of thoughts build during hypomania. This speed increase may range from a very mild quickening to complete psychotic incoherence. It is not yet clear what causes this qualitative change in mental processing. Nevertheless, this altered cognitive state may well facilitate the formation of unique ideas and associations.

People with manic-depressive illness and those who are creatively accomplished share certain noncognitive features: the ability to function well on a few hours of sleep, the focus needed to work intensively, bold and restless attitudes, and an ability to experience a profound depth and variety of emotions. The less dramatic daily aspects of manic-depression might also provide creative advantage to some individuals. The manic-depressive temperament is, in a biological sense, an alert, sensitive system that reacts strongly and swiftly. It responds to the world with a wide range of emotional, perceptual, intellectual, behavioral and energy changes. In a sense, depression is a view of the world through a dark glass, and mania is that seen through a kaleidoscope—often brilliant but fractured.

Where depression questions, ruminates and hesitates, mania answers with vigor and certainty. The constant transitions in and out of constricted and then expansive thoughts, subdued and then violent responses, grim and then ebullient moods, withdrawn and then outgoing stances, cold and then fiery states—and the rapidity and fluidity of moves through such contrasting experiences—can be painful and confusing. Ideally, though, such chaos in those able to

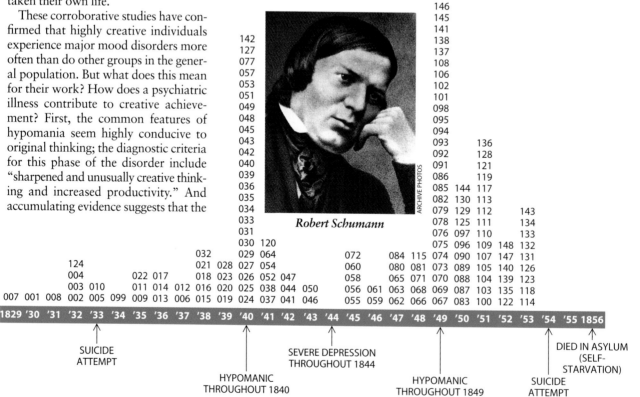

ADAPTED FROM E. SLATER AND A. MEYER, 1959

Robert Schumann ARCHIVE PHOTOS

SUICIDE ATTEMPT

HYPOMANIC THROUGHOUT 1840

SEVERE DEPRESSION THROUGHOUT 1844

HYPOMANIC THROUGHOUT 1849

SUICIDE ATTEMPT

DIED IN ASYLUM (SELF-STARVATION)

ROBERT SCHUMANN'S MUSICAL WORKS, charted by year and opus number (*above*), show a striking relation between his mood states and his productivity. He composed the most when hypomanic and the least when depressed. Both of Schumann's parents were clinically depressed, and two other first-degree relatives committed suicide. Schumann himself attempted suicide twice and died in an insane asylum. One of his sons spent more than 30 years in a mental institution.

Manic-Depressive Illness and Creativity

The Case of Vincent van Gogh

Many clinicians have reviewed the medical and psychiatric problems of the painter Vincent van Gogh posthumously, diagnosing him with a range of disorders, including epilepsy, schizophrenia, digitalis and absinthe poisoning, manic-depressive psychosis, acute intermittent porphyria and Ménière's disease.

Richard Jed Wyatt of the National Institute of Mental Health and I have argued in detail that van Gogh's symptoms, the natural course of his illness and his family psychiatric history strongly indicate manic-depressive illness. The extent of the artist's purported use of absinthe and convulsive behavior remains unclear; in any event, his psychiatric symptoms long predate any possible history of seizures. It is possible that he suffered from both an epileptic disorder and manic-depressive illness. —*K. R. J.*

METROPOLITAN MUSEUM OF ART, GIFT OF ADELE R. LEVY, 1958

Irises, 1889

transcend it or shape it to their will can provide a familiarity with transitions that is probably useful in artistic endeavors. This vantage readily accepts ambiguities and the counteracting forces in nature.

Extreme changes in mood exaggerate the normal tendency to have conflicting selves; the undulating, rhythmic and transitional moods and cognitive changes so characteristic of manic-depressive illness can blend or harness seemingly contradictory moods, observations and perceptions. Ultimately, these fluxes and yokings may reflect truth in humanity and nature more accurately than could a more fixed viewpoint. The "consistent attitude toward life" may not, as Byron scholar Jerome J. McGann of the University of Virginia points out, be as insightful as an ability to live with, and portray, constant change.

The ethical and societal implications of the association between mood disorders and creativity are important but poorly understood. Some treatment strategies pay insufficient heed to the benefits manic-depressive illness can bestow on some individuals. Certainly most manic-depressives seek relief from the disease, and lithium and anticonvulsant drugs are very effective therapies for manias and depressions. Nevertheless, these drugs can dampen a person's general intellect and limit his or her emotional and perceptual range. For this reason, many manic-depressive patients stop taking these medications.

Left untreated, however, manic-depressive illness often worsens over time— and no one is creative when severely depressed, psychotic or dead. The attacks of both mania and depression tend to grow more frequent and more severe. Without regular treatment the disease eventually becomes less responsive to medication. In addition, bipolar and unipolar patients frequently abuse mood-altering substances, such as alcohol and illicit drugs, which can cause secondary medical and emotional burdens for manic-depressive and depressed patients.

The Goal of Treatment

The real task of imaginative, compassionate and effective treatment, therefore, is to give patients more meaningful choices than they are now afforded. Useful intervention must control the extremes of depression and psychosis without sacrificing crucial human emotions and experiences. Given time and increasingly sophisticated research, psychiatrists will likely gain a better understanding of the complex biological basis for mood disorders. Eventually, the development of new drugs should make it possible to treat manic-depressive individuals so that those aspects of temperament and cognition that are essential to the creative process remain intact.

The development of more specific and less problematic therapies should be swift once scientists find the gene, or genes, responsible for the disease. Prenatal tests and other diagnostic measures may then become available; these possi-

bilities raise a host of complicated ethical issues. It would be irresponsible to romanticize such a painful, destructive and all too often deadly disease. Hence, 3 to 5 percent of the Human Genome Project's total budget (which is conservatively estimated at $3 billion) has been set aside for studies of the social, ethical and legal implications of genetic research. It is hoped that these investigations will examine the troubling issues surrounding manic-depression and major depression at length. To help those who have manic-depressive illness, or who are at risk for it, must be a major public health priority. **SA**

Further Reading

TENNYSON: THE UNQUIET HEART. R. B. Martin. Oxford University Press, 1980.

CREATIVITY AND MENTAL ILLNESS: PREVALENCE RATES IN WRITERS AND THEIR FIRST-DEGREE RELATIVES. Nancy C. Andreasen in *American Journal of Psychiatry*, Vol. 144, No. 10, pages 1288-1292; October 1987.

MANIC DEPRESSIVE ILLNESS. Frederick K. Goodwin and Kay R. Jamison. Oxford University Press, 1990.

CREATIVE ACHIEVEMENT AND PSYCHOPATHOLOGY: COMPARISON AMONG PROFESSIONS. Arnold M. Ludwig in *American Journal of Psychiatry*, Vol. 46, No. 3, pages 330–356; July 1992.

TOUCHED WITH FIRE: MANIC-DEPRESSIVE ILLNESS AND THE ARTISTIC TEMPERAMENT. Kay R. Jamison. Free Press/Macmillan, 1993.

Decoding
Schizophrenia

A fuller understanding of signaling in the brain of people with this disorder offers new hope for improved therapy

By Daniel C. Javitt and Joseph T. Coyle

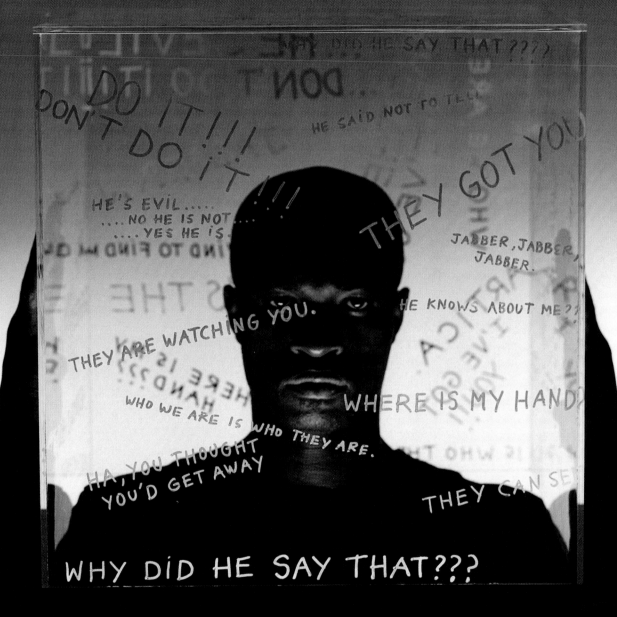

Today the word "schizophrenia" brings to mind

such names as John Nash and Andrea Yates. Nash, the subject of the Oscar-winning film *A Beautiful Mind,* emerged as a mathematical prodigy and eventually won a Nobel Prize for his early work, but he became so profoundly disturbed by the brain disorder in young adulthood that he lost his academic career and floundered for years before recovering. Yates, a mother of five who suffers from both depression and schizophrenia, infamously drowned her young children in a bathtub to "save them from the devil" and is now in prison.

The experiences of Nash and Yates are typical in some ways but atypical in others. Of the roughly 1 percent of the world's population stricken with schizophrenia, most remain largely disabled throughout adulthood. Rather than being geniuses like Nash, many show below-average intelligence even before they become symptomatic and then undergo a further decline in IQ when the illness sets in, typically during young adulthood. Unfortunately, only a minority ever achieve gainful employment. In contrast to Yates, fewer than half marry or raise families. Some 15 percent reside for long periods in state or county mental health facilities, and another 15 percent end up incarcerated for petty crimes and vagrancy. Roughly 60 percent live in poverty, with one in 20 ending up homeless. Because of poor social support, more individuals with schizophrenia become victims than perpetrators of violent crime.

Medications exist but are problematic. The major options today, called antipsychotics, stop all symptoms in only about 20 percent of patients. (Those lucky enough to respond in this way tend to function well as long as they continue treatment; too many, however, abandon their medicines over time, usually because of side effects, a desire to be "normal" or a loss of access to mental health care). Two thirds gain some relief from antipsychotics yet remain symptomatic throughout life, and the remainder show no significant response.

An inadequate arsenal of medications is only one of the obstacles to treating this tragic disorder effectively. Another is the theories guiding drug therapy. Brain cells (neurons) communicate by releasing chemicals called neurotransmitters that either excite or inhibit other neurons. For decades, theories of schizophrenia have focused on a single neurotransmitter: dopamine. In the past few years, though, it has become clear that a disturbance in dopamine levels is just a part of the story and that, for many, the main abnormalities lie elsewhere. In particular, suspicion has fallen on deficiencies in the neurotransmitter glutamate. Scientists now realize that schizophrenia affects virtually all parts of the brain and that, unlike dopamine, which plays an important role only in isolated regions, glutamate is critical virtually everywhere. As a result, investigators are searching for treatments that can reverse the underlying glutamate deficit.

Multiple Symptoms

TO DEVELOP better treatments, investigators need to understand how schizophrenia arises—which means they need to account for all its myriad symptoms. Most of these fall into categories termed "positive," "negative" and "cognitive." Positive symptoms generally imply occurrences beyond normal experience; negative symptoms generally connote diminished experience. Cognitive, or "disorganized," symptoms refer to difficulty maintaining a logical, coherent flow of conversation, maintaining attention, and thinking on an abstract level.

The public is most familiar with the positive symptoms, particularly agitation, paranoid delusions (in which people feel conspired against) and hallucinations, commonly in the form of spoken voices. Command hallucinations, where voices tell people to hurt themselves or others, are an especially ominous sign: they can be difficult to resist and may precipitate violent actions.

The negative and cognitive symptoms are less dramatic but more pernicious. These can include a cluster called the 4 A's: *a*utism (loss of interest in other people or the surroundings), *a*mbivalence (emotional withdrawal), blunted *a*ffect (manifested by a bland and unchanging facial expression), and the cognitive problem of loose *a*ssociation (in which people join thoughts without clear logic, frequently jumbling words together into a meaningless word salad). Other common symptoms include a lack of spontaneity, impoverished speech, difficulty establishing rapport and a slowing of movement. Apathy and disinterest especially can

Overview/*Schizophrenia*

- Scientists have long viewed schizophrenia as arising out of a disturbance in a particular brain system—one in which brain cells communicate using a signaling chemical, or neurotransmitter, called dopamine.
- Yet new research is shifting emphasis from dopamine to another neurotransmitter, glutamate. Impaired glutamate signaling appears to be a major contributor to the disorder.
- Drugs are now in development to treat the illness based on this revised understanding of schizophrenia's underlying causes.

cause friction between patients and their families, who may view these attributes as signs of laziness rather than manifestations of the illness.

When individuals with schizophrenia are evaluated with pencil-and-paper tests designed to detect brain injury, they show a pattern suggestive of widespread dysfunction. Virtually all aspects of brain operation, from the most basic sensory processes to the most complex aspects of thought are affected to some extent. Certain functions, such as the ability to form new memories either temporarily or permanently or to solve complex problems, may be particularly impaired. Patients also display difficulty solving the types of problems encountered in daily living, such as describing what friends are for or what to do if all the lights in the house go out at once. The inability to handle these common problems, more than anything else, accounts for the difficulty such individuals have in living independently. Overall, then, schizophrenia conspires to rob people of the very qualities they need to thrive in society: personality, social skills and wit.

Beyond Dopamine

THE EMPHASIS on dopamine-related abnormalities as a cause of schizophrenia emerged in the 1950s, as a result of the fortuitous discovery that a class of medication called the phenothiazines was able to control the positive symptoms of the disorder. Subsequent studies demonstrated that these substances work by blocking the functioning of a specific group of chemical-sensing molecules called dopamine D2 receptors, which sit on the surface of certain nerve cells and convey dopamine's signals to the cells' interior. At the same time, research led by the recent Nobel laureate Arvid Carlsson revealed that amphetamine, which was known to induce hallucinations and delusions in habitual abusers, stimulated dopamine release in the brain. Together these two findings led to the "dopamine theory," which proposes that most symptoms of schizophrenia stem from excess dopamine release in important brain regions, such as the limbic system (thought to regulate emotion) and the frontal lobes

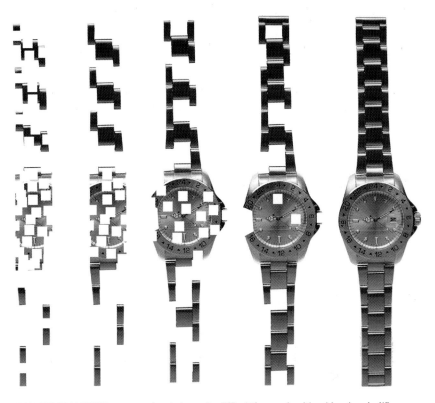

PERCEIVING FRAGMENTS as parts of a whole can be difficult for people with schizophrenia. When normal subjects view fractured images like those above in sequence, they identify the object quickly, but schizophrenic patients often cannot make that leap swiftly.

(thought to regulate abstract reasoning).

Over the past 40 years, both the strengths and limitations of the theory have become apparent. For some patients, especially those with prominent positive symptoms, the theory has proved robust, fitting symptoms and guiding treatment well. The minority of those who display only positive manifestations frequently function quite well—holding jobs, having families and suffering relatively little cognitive decline over time—if they stick with their medicines.

Yet for many, the hypothesis fits poorly. These are the people whose symptoms come on gradually, not dramatically, and in whom negative symptoms overshadow the positive. The sufferers grow withdrawn, often isolating themselves for years. Cognitive functioning is poor, and patients improve slowly, if at all, when treated with even the best existing medications on the market.

Such observations have prompted some researchers to modify the dopamine hypothesis. One revision suggests, for example, that the negative and cognitive symptoms may stem from *reduced* dopamine levels in certain parts of the brain, such as the frontal lobes, and increased dopamine in other parts of the brain, such as the limbic system. Because dopamine receptors in the frontal lobe are primarily of the D1 (rather than D2) variety, in-

THE AUTHORS

DANIEL C. JAVITT and JOSEPH T. COYLE have studied schizophrenia for many years. Javitt is director of the Program in Cognitive Neuroscience and Schizophrenia at the Nathan Kline Institute for Psychiatric Research in Orangeburg, N.Y., and professor of psychiatry at the New York University School of Medicine. His paper demonstrating that the glutamate-blocking drug PCP reproduces the symptoms of schizophrenia was the second-most cited schizophrenia publication of the 1990s. Coyle is Eben S. Draper Professor of Psychiatry and Neuroscience at Harvard Medical School and also editor in chief of the Archives of General Psychiatry. Both authors have won numerous awards for their research. Javitt and Coyle hold independent patents for use of NMDA modulators in the treatment of schizophrenia, and Javitt has significant financial interests in Medifoods and Glytech, companies attempting to develop glycine and D-serine as treatments for schizophrenia.

THE BRAIN IN SCHIZOPHRENIA

MANY BRAIN REGIONS and systems operate abnormally in schizophrenia, including those highlighted below. Imbalances in the neurotransmitter dopamine were once thought to be the prime cause of schizophrenia. But new findings suggest that impoverished signaling by the more pervasive neurotransmitter glutamate—or, more specifically, by one of glutamate's key targets on neurons (the NMDA receptor)—better explains the wide range of symptoms in this disorder.

BASAL GANGLIA
Involved in movement and emotions and in integrating sensory information. Abnormal functioning in schizophrenia is thought to contribute to paranoia and hallucinations. (Excessive blockade of dopamine receptors in the basal ganglia by traditional antipsychotic medicines leads to motor side effects.)

AUDITORY SYSTEM
Enables humans to hear and understand speech. In schizophrenia, overactivity of the speech area (called Wernicke's area) can create auditory hallucinations—the illusion that internally generated thoughts are real voices coming from the outside.

OCCIPITAL LOBE
Processes information about the visual world. People with schizophrenia rarely have full-blown visual hallucinations, but disturbances in this area contribute to such difficulties as interpreting complex images, recognizing motion, and reading emotions on others' faces.

FRONTAL LOBE
Critical to problem solving, insight and other high-level reasoning. Perturbations in schizophrenia lead to difficulty in planning actions and organizing thoughts.

HIPPOCAMPUS
Mediates learning and memory formation, intertwined functions that are impaired in schizophrenia.

LIMBIC SYSTEM
Involved in emotion. Disturbances are thought to contribute to the agitation frequently seen in schizophrenia.

DIFFERENT NEUROTRANSMITTERS, SAME RESULTS

SOME SCIENTISTS have proposed that too much dopamine leads to symptoms emanating from the basal ganglia and that too little dopamine leads to symptoms associated with the frontal cortex. Insufficient glutamate signaling could produce those same symptoms, however.

IN THE REST OF THE CORTEX, glutamate is prevalent, but dopamine is largely absent.

IN THE FRONTAL CORTEX, where dopamine promotes cell firing (by acting on D1 receptors), glutamate's stimulatory signals amplify those of dopamine; hence, a shortage of glutamate would decrease neural activity, just as if too little dopamine were present.

IN THE BASAL GANGLIA, where dopamine normally inhibits cell firing (by acting on D2 receptors on nerve cells), glutamate's stimulatory signals oppose those of dopamine; hence, a shortage of glutamate would increase inhibition, just as if too much dopamine were present.

ALFRED T. KAMAJIAN

vestigators have begun to search, so far unsuccessfully, for medications that stimulate D1 receptors while inhibiting D2s.

In the late 1980s researchers began to recognize that some pharmaceuticals, such as clozapine (Clozaril), were less likely to cause stiffness and other neurologic side effects than older treatments, such as chlorpromazine (Thorazine) or haloperidol (Haldol), and were more effective in treating persistent positive and negative symptoms. Clozapine, known as an atypical antipsychotic, inhibits dopamine receptors less than the older medications and affects the activity of various other neurotransmitters more strongly. Such discoveries led to the development and wide adoption of several newer atypical antipsychotics based on the actions of clozapine (certain of which, unfortunately, now turn out to be capable of causing diabetes and other unexpected side effects). The discoveries also led to the proposal that dopamine was not the only neurotransmitter disturbed in schizophrenia; others were involved as well.

Theories focusing largely on dopamine are problematic on additional grounds. Improper dopamine balance cannot account for why one individual with schizophrenia responds almost completely to treatment, whereas someone else shows no apparent response. Nor can it explain why positive symptoms respond so much better than negative or cognitive ones do. Finally, despite decades of research, investigations of dopamine have yet to uncover a smoking gun. Neither the enzymes that produce this neurotransmitter nor the receptors to which it binds appear sufficiently altered to account for the panoply of observed symptoms.

The Angel Dust Connection

IF DOPAMINE CANNOT account well for schizophrenia, what is the missing link? A critical clue came from the effects of another abused drug: PCP (phencyclidine), also known as angel dust. In contrast to amphetamine, which mimics only the positive symptoms of the disease, PCP induces symptoms that resemble the full range of schizophrenia's manifestations: negative and cognitive and, at times, positive. These effects are seen not just in abusers of PCP but also in individuals given brief, low doses of PCP or ketamine (an anesthetic with similar effects) in controlled drug-challenge trials.

Such studies first drew parallels between the effects of PCP and the symptoms of schizophrenia in the 1960s. They showed, for example, that individuals receiving PCP exhibited the same type of disturbances in interpreting proverbs as those with schizophrenia. More recent studies with ketamine have produced even more compelling similarities. Notably, during ketamine challenge, normal individuals develop difficulty thinking abstractly, learning new information, shifting strategies or placing information in temporary storage. They show a general motor slowing and reduction in speech output just like that seen in schizophrenia. Individuals given PCP or ketamine also grow withdrawn, sometimes even mute; when they talk, they speak tangentially and concretely. PCP and ketamine rarely induce schizophrenialike hallucinations in normal volunteers, but they exacerbate these disturbances in those who already have schizophrenia.

The ability of PCP and ketamine to induce a broad spectrum of schizophrenialike symptoms suggests that these drugs replicate some key molecular disturbance in the brain of schizophrenic patients. At the molecular level the drugs impair the functioning of the brain signaling systems that rely on glutamate, the main excitatory neurotransmitter in the brain. More precisely, they block the action of a form of glutamate receptor known as the NMDA receptor, which plays a critical role in brain development, learning, memory and neural processing in general. This receptor also participates in regulating dopamine release, and blockade of NMDA receptors produces the same disturbances of dopamine function typically seen in schizophrenia. Thus, NMDA receptor dysfunction, by itself, can explain both negative and cognitive symptoms of schizophrenia as well as the dopamine abnormalities at the root of the positive symptoms.

One example of the research implicating NMDA receptors in schizophrenia relates to the way the brain normally pro-

Drug Classes in Development

Unless otherwise noted, the compounds mentioned below are in the early stages of human testing. Their developers or producers are listed in parentheses.

Stimulators of NMDA-type glutamate receptors aim to overcome the signaling deficits that apparently contribute to many schizophrenic symptoms.
Examples: Glycine (Medifoods), D-serine (Glytech). As natural substances, both of them are sold, but they remain under evaluation specifically for their value in treating schizophrenia.

Stimulators of AMPA-type glutamate receptors—also called ampakines—may improve some aspects of memory and cognition in people with schizophrenia.
Example: CX516 (Cortex Pharmaceuticals)

Modulators of another class of glutamate receptors—metabotropic receptors—can regulate glutamate release and potentially restore the balance between the activity of NMDA and AMPA receptors.
Example: LY354740 (Eli Lilly)

Inhibitors of glycine transport reduce glycine removal from synapses, which should increase signaling by NMDA receptors.
Example: GlyT-1 (NPS Pharmaceuticals and Janssen Pharmaceutica)

Stimulators of alpha 7 nicotinic receptors, the same receptors activated by the nicotine in cigarettes, indirectly stimulate the brain's NMDA receptors. Schizophrenics often smoke heavily, probably because the nicotine, acting on alpha 7 receptors, helps them to focus.
Example: DMXB-A (University of Colorado Health Sciences Center)

Stimulators of D1 dopamine receptors are being developed mainly for Parkinson's disease and have passed initial safety trials. They might also correct dopamine deficiencies in schizophrenia, but clinical trials for that purpose have not yet been performed.
Example: ABT-431 (Abbott Laboratories)

cesses information. Beyond strengthening connections between neurons, NMDA receptors amplify neural signals, much as transistors in old-style radios boosted weak radio signals into strong sounds. By selectively amplifying key neural signals, these receptors help the brain respond to some messages and ignore others, thereby facilitating mental focus and attention. Ordinarily, people respond more intensely to sounds presented infrequently than to those presented frequently and to sounds heard while listening than to sounds they make themselves while speaking. But people with schizophrenia do not respond this way, which implies that their brain circuits reliant on NMDA receptors are out of kilter.

If reduced NMDA receptor activity prompts schizophrenia's symptoms, what then causes this reduction? The answer remains unclear. Some reports show that people with schizophrenia have fewer NMDA receptors, although the genes that give rise to the receptors appear unaffected. If NMDA receptors are intact and present in proper amounts, perhaps

the problem lies with a flaw in glutamate release or with a buildup of compounds that disrupt NMDA activity.

Some evidence supports each of these ideas. For instance, postmortem studies of schizophrenic patients reveal not only lower levels of glutamate but also higher levels of two compounds (NAAG and kynurenic acid) that impair the activity of NMDA receptors. Moreover, blood levels of the amino acid homocysteine are elevated; homocysteine, like kynurenic acid, blocks NMDA receptors in the brain. Overall, schizophrenia's pattern of onset and symptoms suggests that chemicals disrupting NMDA receptors may accumulate in sufferers' brains, although the research verdict is not yet in. Entirely different mechanisms may end up explaining why NMDA receptor transmission becomes attenuated.

New Treatment Possibilities

REGARDLESS OF what causes NMDA signaling to go awry in schizophrenia, the new understanding—and preliminary studies in patients—offers hope that drug

therapy can correct the problem. Support for this idea comes from studies showing that clozapine, one of the most effective medications for schizophrenia identified to date, can reverse the behavioral effects of PCP in animals, something that older antipsychotics cannot do. Further, short-term trials with agents known to stimulate NMDA receptors have produced encouraging results. Beyond adding support to the glutamate hypothesis, these results have enabled long-term clinical trials to begin. If proved effective in large-scale tests, agents that activate NMDA receptors will become the first entirely new class of medicines developed specifically to target the negative and cognitive symptoms of the disorder.

The two of us have conducted some of those studies. When we and our colleagues administered the amino acids glycine and D-serine to patients with their standard medications, the subjects showed a 30 to 40 percent decline in cognitive and negative symptoms and some improvement in positive symptoms. Delivery of a medication, D-cycloserine, that is primarily used for treating tuberculosis but happens to cross-react with the NMDA receptor, produced similar results. Based on such findings, the National Institute of Mental Health has organized multicenter clinical trials at four hospitals to determine the effectiveness of D-cycloserine and glycine as therapies for schizophrenia; results should be available this year. Trials of D-serine, which is not yet approved for use in the U.S., are ongoing elsewhere with encouraging preliminary results as well. These agents have also been helpful when taken with the newest generation of atypical antipsychotics, which raises the hope that therapy can be developed to control all three major classes of symptoms at once.

None of the agents tested to date may have the properties needed for commercialization; for instance, the doses required may be too high. We and others are therefore exploring alternative avenues. Molecules that slow glycine's removal from brain synapses—known as glycine transport inhibitors—might enable glycine to stick around longer than usual, thereby increasing stimulation of

Steep Social Costs

SCHIZOPHRENIA, which affects about two million Americans, takes an enormous toll on society. Because it tends to arise in young adulthood and persist, it rings up a huge tally in health care bills and lost wages and ranks among the costliest illnesses in the U.S.

Treatment and strong social support enable some individuals to lead relatively productive and satisfying lives, but most are not so lucky. Fewer than a third can hold a job, and half of those do so only because they have intensive assistance. Men (who tend to become symptomatic earlier than women) usually do not marry, and women who tie the knot frequently enter into marriages that do not last. Because individuals with schizophrenia often isolate themselves and lack jobs, they constitute a disproportionate share of the chronically homeless population.

People with this disorder also have a high likelihood of becoming substance abusers. About 60 percent of symptomatic individuals smoke cigarettes, and half abuse alcohol, marijuana or cocaine. Such activities can lead to poor compliance with treatment and can exacerbate psychotic symptoms, increasing propensities toward violence. (Abstainers, however, behave no more violently than the general population.) Homelessness and substance abuse combine to land many with schizophrenia in prisons and county jails, where they often fail to get the treatment they require.

The grim figures do not end there: roughly 10 percent of people with schizophrenia commit suicide (usually during the illness's early stages), a higher rate than results from major depression. But there is one bright note: clozapine, the atypical antipsychotic introduced in 1989, has recently been shown to reduce the risk of suicide and substance abuse. Whether newer atypical agents exert a similar effect remains to be determined, however.   —D.C.J. and J.T.C.

NMDA receptors. Agents that directly activate "AMPA-type" glutamate receptors, which work in concert with NMDA receptors, are also under active investigation. And agents that prevent the breakdown of glycine or D-serine in the brain have been proposed.

Many Avenues of Attack

SCIENTISTS INTERESTED in easing schizophrenia are also looking beyond signaling systems in the brain to other factors that might contribute to, or protect against, the disorder. For example, investigators have applied so-called gene chips to study brain tissue from people who have died, simultaneously comparing the activity of tens of thousands of genes in individuals with and without schizophrenia. So far they have determined that many genes important to signal transmission across synapses are less active in those with schizophrenia—but exactly what this information says about how the disorder develops or how to treat it is unclear.

Genetic studies in schizophrenia have nonetheless yielded intriguing findings recently. The contribution of heredity to schizophrenia has long been controversial. If the illness were dictated solely by genetic inheritance, the identical twin of a schizophrenic person would always be schizophrenic as well, because the two have the same genetic makeup. In reality, however, when one twin has schizophrenia, the identical twin has about a 50 percent chance of also being afflicted. Moreover, only about 10 percent of first-degree family members (parents, children or siblings) share the illness even though they have on average 50 percent of genes in common with the affected individual. This disparity suggests that genetic inheritance can strongly predispose people to schizophrenia but that environmental factors can nudge susceptible individuals into illness or perhaps shield them from it. Prenatal infections, malnutrition, birth complications and brain injuries are all among the influences suspected of promoting the disorder in genetically predisposed individuals.

Over the past few years, several genes have been identified that appear to increase susceptibility to schizophrenia. In-

OBJECTS often have hidden meanings to people with schizophrenia, who may hoard news items, pictures or other things that would seem useless to others. This wall is a re-creation.

terestingly, one of these genes codes for an enzyme (catechol-O-methyltransferase) involved in the metabolism of dopamine, particularly in the prefrontal cortex. Genes coding for proteins called dysbindin and neuregulin seem to affect the number of NMDA receptors in brain. The gene for an enzyme involved in the breakdown of D-serine (D-amino acid oxidase) may exist in multiple forms, with the most active form producing an approximately fivefold increase in risk for schizophrenia. Other genes may give rise to traits associated with schizophrenia but not the disease itself. Because each gene involved in schizophrenia produces only a small increase in risk, genetic studies must include large numbers of subjects to detect an effect and often generate conflicting results. On the other hand, the existence of multiple genes predisposing for schizophrenia may help explain the variability of symptoms across individuals, with some people perhaps showing the greatest effect in dopamine pathways and others evincing significant involvement of other neurotransmitter pathways.

Finally, scientists are looking for clues by imaging living brains and by comparing brains of people who have died. In general, individuals with schizophrenia have smaller brains than unaffected individuals of similar age and sex. Whereas the deficits were once thought to be restricted to areas such as the brain's frontal lobe, more recent studies have revealed similar abnormalities in many brain regions: those with schizophrenia have abnormal levels of brain response while performing tasks that activate not only the frontal lobes but also other areas of the brain, such as those that control auditory and visual processing. Perhaps the most important finding to come out of recent research is that no one area of the brain is "responsible" for schizophrenia. Just as normal behavior requires the concerted action of the entire brain, the disruption of function in schizophrenia must be seen as a breakdown in the sometimes subtle interactions both within and between different brain regions.

Because schizophrenia's symptoms vary so greatly, many investigators believe that multiple factors probably cause the syndrome. What physicians diagnose as schizophrenia today may prove to be a cluster of different illnesses, with similar and overlapping symptoms. Nevertheless, as researchers more accurately discern the syndrome's neurological bases, they should become increasingly skilled at developing treatments that adjust brain signaling in the specific ways needed by each individual. ∎

MORE TO EXPLORE

Recent Advances in the Phencyclidine Model of Schizophrenia. D. C. Javitt and S. R. Zukin in *American Journal of Psychiatry,* Vol. 148, No. 10, pages 1301–1308; October 1991.

Efficacy of High-Dose Glycine in the Treatment of Enduring Negative Symptoms of Schizophrenia. U. Heresco-Levy, D. C. Javitt, M. Ermilov, C. Mordel, G. Silipo and M. Lichtenstein in *Archives of General Psychiatry,* Vol. 56, No. 1, pages 29–36; January 1999.

A Beautiful Mind: The Life of Mathematical Genius and Nobel Laureate John Nash. Sylvia Nasar. Touchstone Books, 2001.

The Emerging Role of Glutamate in the Pathophysiology and Treatment of Schizophrenia. D. C. Goff and J. T. Coyle in *American Journal of Psychiatry,* Vol. 158, No. 9, pages 1367–1377; September 2001.

Revolution #9. Directed by Tim McCann. Wellspring Media, 2001. VHS and DVD release, 2003.

By Robert B. Cialdini

the SCIENCE of Persuasion

Social psychology has determined the basic principles that govern getting to "yes"

Hello there.

I hope you've enjoyed the magazine so far. Now I'd like to let you in on something of great importance to you personally. Have you ever been tricked into saying yes? Ever felt trapped into buying something you didn't really want or contributing to some suspicious-sounding cause? And have you ever wished you understood why you acted in this way so that you could withstand these clever ploys in the future?

Yes? Then clearly this article is just right for you. It contains valuable information on the most powerful psychological pressures that get you to say yes to requests. And it's chock-full of NEW, IMPROVED *research showing exactly how and why these techniques work. So don't delay, just settle in and get the information that, after all, you've already agreed you want.*

The scientific study of the process of social influence has been under way for well over half a century, beginning in earnest with the propaganda, public information and persuasion programs of World War II. Since that time, numerous social scientists have investigated the ways in which one individual can influence another's attitudes and actions. For the past 30 years, I have participated in that endeavor, concentrating primarily on the major factors that bring about a specific form of behavior change—compliance with a request. Six basic tendencies of human behavior come into play in generating a positive response: recip-rocation, consistency, social validation, liking, authority and scarcity. As these six tendencies help to govern our business dealings, our societal involvements and our personal relationships, knowledge of the rules of persuasion can truly be thought of as empowerment.

Reciprocation

When the Disabled American Veterans organization mails out requests for contributions, the appeal succeeds only about 18 percent of the time. But when the mailing includes a set of free personalized address labels, the success rate almost doubles, to 35 percent. To understand the effect of

STEVEN ADAMS AP Photo/Tribune-Review

the unsolicited gift, we must recognize the reach and power of an essential rule of human conduct: the code of reciprocity.

All societies subscribe to a norm that obligates individuals to repay in kind what they have received. Evolutionary selection pressure has probably entrenched the behavior in social animals such as ourselves. The demands of reciprocity begin to explain the boost in donations to the veterans group. Receiving a gift—unsolicited and perhaps even unwanted—convinced significant numbers of potential donors to return the favor.

Charitable organizations are far from alone in taking this approach: food stores offer free samples, exterminators offer free in-home inspections,

health clubs offer free workouts. Customers are thus exposed to the product or service, but they are also indebted. Consumers are not the only ones who fall under the sway of reciprocity. Pharmaceutical companies spend millions of dollars every year to support medical researchers and to provide gifts to individual physicians—activities that may subtly influence investigators' findings and physicians' recommendations. A 1998 study in the *New England Journal of Medicine* found that only 37 percent of researchers who published conclusions critical of the safety of calcium channel blockers had previously received drug company support. Among those whose conclusions attested to the drugs' safety, however, the number of

Free samples carry a subtle price tag; they psychologically indebt the consumer to reciprocate. Here shoppers get complimentary tastes of a new product, green ketchup.

Public commitment of signing a petition influences the signer to behave consistently with that position in the future.

those who had received free trips, research funding or employment skyrocketed—to 100 percent.

Reciprocity includes more than gifts and favors; it also applies to concessions that people make to one another. For example, assume that you reject my large request, and I then make a concession to you by retreating to a smaller request. You may very well then reciprocate with a concession of your own: agreement with my lesser request. In the mid-1970s my colleagues and I conducted an experiment that clearly illustrates the dynamics of reciprocal concessions. We stopped a random sample of passersby on public walkways and asked them if they would volunteer to chaperone juvenile detention center inmates on a day trip to the zoo. As expected, very few complied, only 17 percent.

For another random sample of passersby, however, we began with an even larger request: to serve as an unpaid counselor at the center for two hours per week for the next two years. Everyone in this second sampling rejected the extreme appeal. At that point we offered them a concession. "If you can't do that," we asked, "would you chaperone a group of juvenile detention center inmates on a day trip to the zoo?" Our concession powerfully stimulated return concessions. The compliance rate nearly tripled, to 50 percent, compared with the straightforward zoo-trip request.

Consistency

In 1998 Gordon Sinclair, the owner of a well-known Chicago restaurant, was struggling with a problem that afflicts all restaurateurs. Patrons frequently reserve a table but, without notice, fail to appear. Sinclair solved the problem by asking his receptionist to change two words of what she said to callers requesting reservations. The change dropped his no-call, no-show rate from 30 to 10 percent immediately.

The two words were effective because they commissioned the force of another potent human motivation: the desire to be, and to appear, consistent. The receptionist merely modified her request from "Please call if you have to change your plans" to "Will you please call if you have to change your plans?" At that point, she politely paused and waited for a response. The wait was pivotal because it induced customers to fill the pause with a public commitment. And public commitments, even seemingly minor ones, direct future action.

In another example, Joseph Schwarzwald of

Bar-Ilan University in Israel and his co-workers nearly doubled monetary contributions for the handicapped in certain neighborhoods. The key factor: two weeks before asking for contributions, they got residents to sign a petition supporting the handicapped, thus making a public commitment to that same cause.

Social Validation

On a wintry morning in the late 1960s, a man stopped on a busy New York City sidewalk and gazed skyward for 60 seconds, at nothing in particular. He did so as part of an experiment by City University of New York social psychologists Stanley Milgram, Leonard Bickman and Lawrence Berkowitz that was designed to find out what effect this action would have on passersby. Most simply detoured or brushed by; 4 percent joined the man in looking up. The experiment was then repeated with a slight change. With the modification, large numbers of pedestrians were induced to come to a halt, crowd together and peer upward.

The single alteration in the experiment incorporated the phenomenon of social validation. One fundamental way that we decide what to do in a situation is to look to what others are doing or have done there. If many individuals have decided in favor of a particular idea, we are more likely to follow, because we perceive the idea to be more correct, more valid.

Milgram, Bickman and Berkowitz introduced the influence of social validation into their street experiment simply by having five men rather than one look up at nothing. With the larger initial set of upward gazers, the percentage of New Yorkers who followed suit more than quadrupled, to 18 percent. Bigger initial sets of planted up-lookers generated an even greater response: a starter group of 15 led 40 percent of passersby to join in, nearly stopping traffic within one minute.

Taking advantage of social validation, requesters can stimulate our compliance by demonstrating (or merely implying) that others just like us have already complied. For example, a study found that a fund-raiser who showed homeowners a list of neighbors who had donated to a local charity significantly increased the frequency of contributions; the longer the list, the greater the effect. Marketers, therefore, go out of their way to inform us when their product is the largest-selling or fastest-growing of its kind, and television commercials regularly depict crowds rushing to stores to acquire the advertised item.

Less obvious, however, are the circumstances under which social validation can backfire to pro-duce the opposite of what a requester intends. An example is the understandable but potentially misguided tendency of health educators to call attention to a problem by depicting it as regrettably frequent. Information campaigns stress that alcohol and drug use is intolerably high, that adolescent suicide rates are alarming and that polluters are spoiling the environment. Although the claims are both true and well intentioned, the creators of these campaigns have missed something basic about the compliance process. Within the statement "Look at all the people who are doing this *undesirable* thing" lurks the powerful and undercutting message "Look at all the people who *are* doing this undesirable thing." Research shows that, as a consequence, many such programs boomerang, generating even more of the undesirable behavior.

For instance, a suicide intervention program administered to New Jersey teenagers informed them of the high number of teenage suicides. Health researcher David Shaffer and his colleagues at Columbia University found that participants became significantly more likely to see suicide as a potential solution to their problems. Of greater effectiveness are campaigns that honestly depict the unwanted activity as damaging despite the fact that relatively few individuals engage in it.

Liking

"Affinity," "rapport" and "affection" all describe a feeling of connection between people. But the simple word "liking" most faithfully captures the concept and has become the standard designation in the social science literature. People prefer to say yes to those they like. Consider the worldwide success of the Tupperware Corporation and its "home party" program. Through the in-home demonstration get-together, the company arranges for its customers to buy from a liked friend, the host, rather than from an unknown salesperson. So favorable has been the effect on proceeds that, according to company literature, a Tupperware party begins somewhere in the world every two seconds. In fact, 75 percent of all Tupperware parties today occur outside the individualistic U.S., in countries where group social bonding is even more important than it is here.

Of course, most commercial transactions take place beyond the homes of friends. Under these much more typical circumstances, those who wish to commission the power of liking employ tactics clustered around certain factors that research has shown to work.

Physical attractiveness can be such a tool. In a

Gross National Product.

This year Americans will produce more litter and pollution than ever before.

If you don't do something about it, who will?

Give A Hoot. Don't Pollute.

Forest Service-USDA

Social validation takes advantage of peer pressure to drive human behavior. Poorly applied, however, it can also undermine attempts to curtail deleterious activities, by pointing out their ubiquity: If everyone's doing it, why shouldn't I?

FOREST SERVICE-USDA

1993 study conducted by Peter H. Reingen of Arizona State University and Jerome B. Kernan, now at George Mason University, good-looking fundraisers for the American Heart Association generated nearly twice as many donations (42 versus 23 percent) as did other requesters. In the 1970s researchers Michael G. Efran and E.W.J. Patterson of the University of Toronto found that voters in Canadian federal elections gave physically attractive candidates several times as many votes as unattractive ones. Yet such voters insisted that their choices would never be influenced by something as superficial as appearance.

Similarity also can expedite the development of rapport. Salespeople often search for, or outright fabricate, a connection between themselves and their customers: "Well, no kidding, you're from Minneapolis? I went to school in Minnesota!" Fund-raisers do the same, with good results. In 1994 psychologists R. Kelly Aune of the University of Hawaii at Manoa and Michael D. Basil of the University of Denver reported research in which solicitors canvassed a college campus asking for contributions to a charity. When the phrase "I'm a student, too" was added to the requests, the amount of the donations more than doubled.

Compliments also stimulate liking, and direct salespeople are trained in the use of praise. Indeed, even inaccurate praise may be effective. Research at the University of North Carolina at Chapel Hill found that compliments produced just as much liking for the flatterer when they were untrue as when they were genuine.

(Are we then doomed to be helplessly manipulated by these principles? No.)

Cooperation is another factor that has been shown to enhance positive feelings and behavior. Salespeople, for example, often strive to be perceived by their prospects as cooperating partners. Automobile sales managers frequently cast themselves as "villains" so the salesperson can "do battle" on the customer's behalf. The gambit naturally leads to a desirable form of liking by the customer for the salesperson, which promotes sales.

Authority

Recall the man who used social validation to get large numbers of passersby to stop and stare at the sky. He might achieve the opposite effect and spur stationary strangers into motion by assuming the mantle of authority. In 1955 University of Texas at Austin researchers Monroe Lefkowitz, Robert R. Blake and Jane S. Mouton discovered that a man could increase by 350 percent the number of pedestrians who would follow him across the street against the light by changing one simple thing. Instead of casual dress, he donned markers of authority: a suit and tie.

Those touting their experience, expertise or scientific credentials may be trying to harness the power of authority: "Babies are our business, our only business," "Four out of five doctors recommend," and so on. (The author's biography on the opposite page in part serves such a purpose.) There is nothing wrong with such claims when they are real, because we usually want the opinions of true authorities. Their insights help us choose quickly and well.

The problem comes when we are subjected to phony claims. If we fail to think, as is often the case when confronted by authority symbols, we can easily be steered in the wrong direction by ersatz experts—those who merely present the aura of legitimacy. That Texas jaywalker in a suit and tie was no more an authority on crossing the street

Behold the power of authority. Certainly not lost on the National Rifle Association is that the authority inherent in such heroic figures as Moses, El Cid and Ben-Hur is linked to the actor who portrayed them, Charlton Heston.

RIC FELD AP Photo

TUPPERWARE (1958) AP Photo

than the rest of the pedestrians who nonetheless followed him. A highly successful ad campaign in the 1970s featured actor Robert Young proclaiming the health benefits of decaffeinated coffee. Young seems to have been able to dispense this medical opinion effectively because he represented, at the time, the nation's most famous physician. That Marcus Welby, M.D., was only a character on a TV show was less important than the appearance of authority.

Scarcity

While at Florida State University in the 1970s, psychologist Stephen West noted an odd occurrence after surveying students about the campus cafeteria cuisine: ratings of the food rose significantly from the week before, even though there had been no change in the menu, food quality or preparation. Instead the shift resulted from an announcement that because of a fire, cafeteria meals would not be available for several weeks.

This account highlights the effect of perceived scarcity on human judgment. A great deal of evidence shows that items and opportunities become more desirable to us as they become less available.

For this reason, marketers trumpet the unique benefits or the one-of-a-kind character of their offerings. It is also for this reason that they consistently engage in "limited time only" promotions or put us into competition with one another using sales campaigns based on "limited supply."

Less widely recognized is that scarcity affects the value not only of commodities but of information as well. Information that is exclusive is more persuasive. Take as evidence the dissertation data of a former student of mine, Amram Knishinsky, who owned a company that imported beef into the U.S. and sold it to supermarkets. To examine the effects of scarcity and exclusivity on compliance, he instructed his telephone sales-

Friends (who are already liked) are powerful salespeople, as Tupperware Corporation discovered. Strangers can co-opt the trappings of friendship to encourage compliance.

(The Author)

ROBERT B. CIALDINI is Regents' Professor of Psychology at Arizona State University, where he has also been named Distinguished Graduate Research Professor. He is past president of the Society of Personality and Social Psychology. Cialdini's book *Influence,* which was the result of a three-year study of the reasons why people comply with requests in everyday settings, has appeared in numerous editions and been published in nine languages. He attributes his longstanding interest in the intricacies of influence to the fact that he was raised in an entirely Italian family, in a predominantly Polish neighborhood, in a historically German city (Milwaukee), in an otherwise rural state.

people to call a randomly selected sample of customers and to make a standard request of them to purchase beef. He also instructed the salespeople to do the same with a second random sample of customers but to add that a shortage of Australian beef was anticipated, which was true, because of certain weather conditions there. The added information that Australian beef was soon to be scarce more than doubled purchases.

Finally, he had his staff call a third sample of customers, to tell them (1) about the impending shortage of Australian beef and (2) that this information came from his company's *exclusive* sources in the Australian national weather service. These customers increased their orders by more than 600 percent. They were influenced by a scarcity double whammy: not only was the beef scarce, but the information that the beef was scarce was itself scarce.

Knowledge Is Power

I think it noteworthy that many of the data presented in this article have come from studies of the practices of persuasion professionals—the marketers, advertisers, salespeople, fund-raisers and their comrades whose financial well-being de-

(Influence across Cultures)

Do the six key factors in the social influence process operate similarly across national boundaries? Yes, but with a wrinkle. The citizens of the world are human, after all, and susceptible to the fundamental tendencies that characterize all members of our species. Cultural norms, traditions and experiences can, however, modify the weight that is brought to bear by each factor.

Consider the results of a report published in 2000 by Stanford University's Michael W. Morris, Joel M. Podolny and Sheira Ariel, who studied employees of Citibank, a multinational financial corporation. The researchers selected four societies for examination: the U.S., China, Spain and Germany. They surveyed Citibank branches within each country and measured employees' willingness to comply voluntarily with a request from a co-worker for assistance with a task. Although multiple key factors could come into play, the main reason employees felt obligated to comply differed in the four nations. Each of these reasons incorporated a different fundamental principle of social influence.

Employees in the U.S. took a reciprocation-based approach to the decision to comply. They asked the question, "What has this person done for me recently?" and felt obligated to volunteer if they owed the requester a favor. Chinese employees responded primarily to authority, in the form of loyalties to those of high status within their small group. They asked, "Is this requester connected to someone in my unit, especially someone who is high-ranking?" If the answer was yes, they felt required to yield.

Spanish Citibank personnel based the deci-

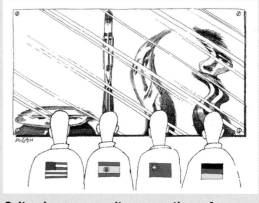

Cultural norms can alter perceptions of persuasion tactics.

sion to comply mostly on liking/friendship. They were willing to help on the basis of friendship norms that encourage faithfulness to one's friends, regardless of position or status. They asked, "Is this requester connected to my friends?" If the answer was yes, they were especially likely to want to comply.

German employees were most compelled by consistency, offering assistance in order to be consistent with the rules of the organization. They decided whether to comply by asking, "According to official regulations and categories, am I supposed to assist this requester?" If the answer was yes, they felt a strong obligation to grant the request.

In sum, although all human societies seem to play by the same set of influence rules, the weights assigned to the various rules can differ across cultures. Persuasive appeals to audiences in distinct cultures need to take such differences into account. —*R.B.C.*

pends on their ability to get others to say yes. A kind of natural selection operates on these people, as those who use unsuccessful tactics soon go out of business. In contrast, those using procedures that work well will survive, flourish and pass on these successful strategies [see "The Power of Memes," by Susan Blackmore; SCIENTIFIC AMERICAN, October 2000]. Thus, over time, the most effective principles of social influence will appear in the repertoires of long-standing persuasion professions. My own work indicates that those principles embody the six fundamental human tendencies examined in this article: reciprocation, consistency, social validation, liking, authority and scarcity.

From an evolutionary point of view, each of the behaviors presented would appear to have been selected for in animals, such as ourselves, that must find the best ways to survive while living in social groups. And in the vast majority of cases, these principles counsel us correctly. It usually makes great sense to repay favors, behave consistently, follow the lead of similar others, favor the requests of those we like, heed legitimate authorities and value scarce resources. Consequently, influence agents who use these principles honestly do us a favor. If an advertising agency, for instance, focused an ad campaign on the genuine weight of authoritative, scientific evidence favoring its client's headache product, all the right people would profit—the agency, the manufacturer *and* the audience. Not so, however, if the agency, finding no particular scientific merit in the pain reliever, "smuggles" the authority principle into the situation through ads featuring actors wearing white lab coats.

Are we then doomed to be helplessly manipulated by these principles? No. By understanding persuasion techniques, we can begin to recognize strategies and thus truly analyze requests and offerings. Our task must be to hold persuasion professionals accountable for the use of the six powerful motivators and to purchase their products and services, support their political proposals or donate to their causes only when they have acted truthfully in the process.

If we make this vital distinction in our dealings with practitioners of the persuasive arts, we will rarely allow ourselves be tricked into assent. Instead we will give ourselves a much better option: to be informed into saying yes. Moreover, as long as we apply the same distinction to our own attempts to influence others, we can legitimately commission the six principles. In seeking to persuade by pointing to the presence of genuine ex-

pertise, growing social validation, pertinent commitments or real opportunities for cooperation, and so on, we serve the interests of both parties and enhance the quality of the social fabric in the bargain.

Surely, someone with your splendid intellect can see the unique benefits of this article. And because you look like a helpful person who would want to share such useful information, let me make a request. Would you buy this issue of the magazine for 10 of your friends? Well, if you can't do that, would you show it to just one friend? Wait, don't answer yet. Because I genuinely like you, I'm going to throw in—at absolutely no extra cost—a set of references that you can consult to learn more about this little-known topic.

Now, will you voice your commitment to help?... Please recognize that I am pausing politely here. But while I'm waiting, I want you to feel totally assured that many others just like you will certainly consent. And I love that shirt you're wearing.

Limited offer of toys available for a short time often creates a figurative feeding frenzy at local fast-food establishments. Scarcity can be manufactured to make a commodity appear more desirable.

PETER BARRERAS AP Photo

(Further Reading)

◆ **Bargaining for Advantage.** G. Richard Shell. Viking, 1999.
◆ **Age of Propaganda: The Everyday Use and Abuse of Persuasion.** Revised edition. A. J. Pratkanis and E. Aronson. W. H. Freeman and Company, 2001.
◆ **Influence: Science and Practice.** Fourth edition. Robert B. Cialdini. Allyn & Bacon, 2001.
◆ **The Power of Persuasion: How We're Bought and Sold.** Robert Levine. John Wiley & Sons, 2003.
◆ For regularly updated information about the social influence process, visit **www.influenceatwork.com**

This psychology reader
is the product of a partnership between
WORTH PUBLISHERS and
SCIENTIFIC AMERICAN.

www.worthpublishers.com

www.sciam.com

ABOUT DAVID G. MYERS

David G. Myers is professor of psychology at
Michigan's Hope College, where he has spent his
career and been voted "outstanding professor" by
students. His writings have appeared in more than
four dozen journals and magazines, from SCIENCE to
SCIENTIFIC AMERICAN, and in a dozen books.

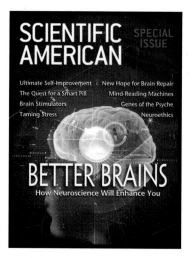

ABOUT SCIENTIFIC AMERICAN

SCIENTIFIC AMERICAN, the oldest continuously
published magazine in the U.S., has brought its
readers unique insights about developments in
science and technology for more than 150 years.

ISBN 0-7167-2416-2

COVER ART: © LAURA JAMES
Used by permission.